Advance Praise

After the Exodus is a refreshing addition to the literature of Rohingya camps in Bangladesh. The feminist lens that the book uses is very useful in casting light on the everyday lives of women. Through intense ethnographic details, life in the camps – the way that families regroup, new relationships formed, the problems with bringing up children in these cramped conditions, the issues surrounding marriage negotiations – are brought to life in vivid detail. The author has indeed successfully drawn us into the intricacies of negotiations that accompany these processes, as well as the fresh ways of problem solving that are brought into play.

Firdous Azim, Professor and Chair at the Department of English and Humanities at BRAC University, Dhaka

This extraordinary monograph weaves the politics of storytelling in the context of acutely gendered violence and ethnic cleansing among Rohingya people with the futures they forge as they remake 'home' in the refugee camps of Bangladesh. Rahman's exquisite research has clearly earned the trust of her informants, and reveals the horrid death and sexual violence against the Rohingya by the Burmese military during what is often a forgotten humanitarian disaster of dispossession and genocide, but also the ways people are remaking home in a new place. This reflexive and original feminist ethnography grapples with the unspeakable crimes against humanity faced by the Rohingya, but goes well beyond their survival in the camps of Cox's Bazaar in Bangladesh, highlighting their presence, perseverance, and strength under conditions not of their own making.

Jennifer Hyndman, author of *Managing Displacement: Refugees and the Politics of Humanitarianism* (2000)

This book provides a much-needed in-depth and poignant examination of the experiences of Rohingya women in the refugee camps of Bangladesh, exploring the complex interplay of gender identity, relations, and roles amid the harsh realities of forced displacement. Rahman restores women as resilient social agents navigating and negotiating patriarchal structures, rather than writing off their experiences as being those of victims unable to attend to their own wellbeing. Her unique approach instead emphasizes the resilience and creative strategies deployed by the Rohingya women to reconstruct their lives and communities, chief among them being the 'Majhee' system. This refreshing focus on the quotidian aspects of life in the camps provides an insightful and much-needed contribution to our understanding of refugee experiences more broadly and of refugee women specifically. Overall, a brilliantly researched and compelling book that offers a crucial perspective on the world's most marginalized individuals, making it a highly relevant and significant read.

Azeem Ibrahim OBE, author of *The Rohingyas: Inside Myanmar's Hidden Genocide* (2016)

After the Exodus

After the Exodus examines how forced migration of the Rohingya from Myanmar to Bangladesh has affected the gendered subjectivities and lived experiences of Rohingya refugee women, and transformed gender relations and roles in displacement. Based on 14 months of feminist ethnographic fieldwork in Bangladesh's Kutupalong-Balukhali refugee camp in 2017 and 2018, the book uncovers the everyday strategies employed by refugee women to create a sense of belonging and to make a life for themselves after forced migration. Rohingya women adapt to camp life by negotiating marriage and intimate experiences, adjusting to changing gender divisions of labour, and navigating encounters with humanitarian aid agencies and male camp leaders. These women strategically bargain shifting power relations to reconstruct their lives in displacement, thereby reclaiming agency and asserting their identity through the spaces they create, inhabit, and reshape; the coping mechanisms they employ; and the bonds of kinship and community they forge.

Farhana Afrin Rahman is currently a Leverhulme Early Career Fellow and Isaac Newton Trust Fellow at the Department of Politics and International Studies, University of Cambridge, and a Junior Research Fellow at Wolfson College, Cambridge. Her research interests include gender, refugees and forced migration, international development, lived experiences, and violence and conflict, amongst others.

SOUTH ASIA IN THE SOCIAL SCIENCES

South Asia has become a laboratory for devising new institutions and practices of modern social life. Forms of capitalist enterprise, providing welfare and social services, the public role of religion, the management of ethnic conflict, popular culture and mass democracy in the countries of the region have shown a marked divergence from known patterns in other parts of the world. South Asia is now being studied for its relevance to the general theoretical understanding of modernity itself.

South Asia in the Social Sciences features books that offer innovative research on contemporary South Asia. It focuses on the place of the region in the various global disciplines of the social sciences and highlight research that uses unconventional sources of information and novel research methods. While recognising that most current research is focused on the larger countries, the series attempts to showcase research on the smaller countries of the region.

After the Exodus

*Gender and Belonging in Bangladesh's
Rohingya Refugee Camps*

Farhana Afrin Rahman

CAMBRIDGE
UNIVERSITY PRESS

Shaftesbury Road, Cambridge CB2 8EA, United Kingdom

One Liberty Plaza, 20th Floor, New York, NY 10006, USA

477 Williamstown Road, Port Melbourne, VIC 3207, Australia

314–321, 3rd Floor, Plot 3, Splendor Forum, Jasola District Centre, New Delhi – 110025, India

103 Penang Road, #05–06/07, Visioncrest Commercial, Singapore 238467

Cambridge University Press is part of Cambridge University Press & Assessment, a department of the University of Cambridge.

We share the University's mission to contribute to society through the pursuit of education, learning and research at the highest international levels of excellence.

www.cambridge.org
Information on this title: www.cambridge.org/9781009414821

First published 2024

Printed in India by Thomson Press India Ltd.

A catalogue record for this publication is available from the British Library

ISBN 978-1-009-41482-1 Hardback

For my parents,
Wahidur Rahman and Ferdousi Begum

Contents

Acknowledgements

Bismillah.

Above all else, all Praise and Glory is due to Allah, whose infinite Mercy and Blessings has led me to see this book through to completion, *alhamdulillah*.

This book is my humble attempt to remember and honour the victims of the devastating Rohingya genocide and stand in solidarity with the survivors – some of whom are now my dearest friends. It is the voices and stories of my Rohingya friends and interlocutors that have breathed life into this book. Though I cannot directly name them, their words, love, warmth, and strength are the lifeblood of this work. We have laughed, cried, sang, and danced together, and I pray that we will continue to do so until our last days. I remember the day one of my Rohingya friends told me: 'the world has forgotten us.' I hope with my humble attempt at sharing their voices and stories, the world will once again remember them. I am only the messenger, but I pray that I have done justice to the gravity of their words, narratives, and everyday lived experiences, *inshaAllah*.

*

First, this book was borne out of my PhD dissertation at the University of Cambridge and for that I must thank my dear supervisor, Manali Desai. I am immensely grateful to her for guiding me through the difficult days of my PhD. She has truly been a caring and committed mentor. I also cannot express enough my deepest gratitude to Jude Browne at the University of Cambridge Centre for Gender Studies for being an amazing pillar of support and guidance throughout my years at the Centre. I am grateful to several funding bodies who supported this research, especially the Cambridge International Trust, the Social Sciences and Humanities Research Council of Canada, the Canadian Centennial Scholarship Fund, among several others.

My thanks also to Wolfson College, Cambridge, where I have been a Junior Research Fellow, the Leverhulme Trust for the Leverhulme Early Career Fellowship at the University of Cambridge, and the Japan Society for the Promotion of Science for the Postdoctoral Fellowship at the University of Tokyo – all these opportunities have been invaluable in helping me focus on turning my PhD dissertation into this book. I am also grateful for my time as a fellow at the Centre for Asia-Pacific Refugee Studies at the University of Auckland and at the Harvard University Asia Center.

For my PhD dissertation, I am very honoured to have received the Special Accolade 'Most Accessible and Captivating Work for the Non-Specialist Reader' and being shortlisted for 'Best Dissertation in the Social Sciences' – both by the International Convention of Asia Scholars Book Prize, 2023. These accolades gave me much-needed encouragement to turn the dissertation into this manuscript. Throughout the editorial and publication process of this book, I am immensely grateful to Anwesha Rana from Cambridge University Press (CUP) for believing in this project and guiding me through various stages of it. Thanks also to Priya Das, Saniya Puri, and Qudsiya Ahmed from CUP for their support.

My deepest thanks to my research assistants and friends in Bangladesh, Zia and Munni, for being incredible sources of support and comfort throughout my time in the refugee camps – their enthusiasm, patience, and friendship helped me accomplish much more than I could have ever imagined. Thanks also to Mohiuddin Uncle and Ahsan Uncle whose help in Bangladesh was invaluable in so many ways.

I am forever grateful for the friendship of many dear people over the years and across several continents from different stages of my life, particularly Nurul Huda Mohd. Razif, Fatema Nakhuda, Nameera Shariff, Marzan Adel, Samia Liaquat, Callie Vandewiele, Laura Caballe-Climent, Hakan Sandal-Wilson, and Sharmila Parmanand.

*

On a more personal note, I dedicate this book to the two strongest, most selfless, and most loving people that have given up so much in this world to make sure their four daughters could achieve anything and everything they never had the opportunity to – my parents, Wahidur Rahman and Ferdousi Begum. They have always encouraged my dreams and never made me feel there was nothing I could not do or achieve. From a young age, they instilled in me a love for travel and adventure, as well as the importance of education that works to make a difference in society. Their countless *du'a*s, unconditional love, guidance, and encouragement have been the biggest blessings, and their hard work and innumerable sacrifices are the reason I am here today. Every single thing I have ever achieved and any success that I have attained is because of their unfailing belief in me. I dedicate this book to them.

My deepest love and gratitude also to the most loving parents-in-law a girl could ever ask for – Masudul Alam Choudhury and Nuzhat Choudhury.

I am blessed to have another set of parents who constantly love, nurture, and encourage me in all of my aspirations. It is because of their relentless *du'a*s that all of this has been possible.

My love and thanks to my sisters Nazneen, Sharmin, and Bushra for always being there – when they say sisters make the best of friends, they were absolutely correct. Thanks also to my brothers-in-law, Ehsan and Muammar, for being the coolest members of our big, crazy family. And of course, my sweetest nieces and nephews – Safa, Siyam, Saad, Yusra, Idris, and Sanaa – who are the absolute lights of my life.

My sincere thanks also to all my aunts, uncles, and cousins in Bangladesh, Japan, and beyond who were incredibly helpful throughout fieldwork and the writing up process.

Finally, and most importantly, none of this would be possible without my husband, Nafay Choudhury, and my little boy, Ilyas Muhammad Choudhury. Nafay has been the best partner, husband, and biggest cheerleader anyone could ask for. The most giving, most loving, and most patient man who unfailingly supports all of my goals, lifts me up every single day to help fight my inner battles, and who has emotionally anchored me through the most difficult and darkest days. I would not have been able to do any of this without him by my side. And to my baby Ilyas, who came in the midst of writing this book – my greatest blessing, joy, and the sweetest little boy in the entire universe. I am at a loss every day of how blessed I am – and what a privilege it is – to be the mother of the kindest, happiest, and most gentle child. There is nothing more important in this world than him. I am so thankful for my little family – Allah has truly blessed me with the best from amongst his most beloved.

There were only 10 minutes left until the *adhan* (call to prayer) for Maghrib (evening prayer). The evening twilight had spread across the horizon beyond the sprawling mass of bamboo and tarp shelters carved into the hillsides of southeastern Bangladesh. The sky blazed with hues of orange and red; the fleeting colours of dusk began to fade away on that hot summer evening in August 2017. We – Absar the driver, my research assistants and friends Munni and Zia, and myself – sat in a rusty old Toyota on our way towards Balukhali refugee camp from the nearby Kutupalong camp. Gathering dust along the way, the car was slowed down by passing *tomtom*s (auto-rickshaws) that weaved in and out of the dirt road as we drove past rows upon rows of tightly packed shelters – their orange and blue tarpaulin tents almost unnoticeable as darkness quietly descended.

We reached Balukhali at 6:30 p.m. as darkness started creeping into the alleyways of the camp. I noticed a group of young boys kicking a limp football in the dusty open space that served as a makeshift parking spot. For these kids, this sandy spot had become their stadium, where they could enter a world of respite and aspiration – if only temporarily – to escape the destitution and bleakness that hung like a cloud over the camps. Another group of children playfully made jokes and began to disperse back towards their homes. While Absar and Zia stayed behind in the car, Munni and I made our way through the city of tents, climbing up small hills up to 30 metres high, past food vendors – often local Bangladeshis from neighbouring villages who had found new economic opportunity from the waves of refugees and non-governmental organizations (NGOs) that had entered their once-pristine locale – closing up shop for the night and groups of men in white *panjabi*s (a traditional pant and shirt outfit) and colourfully checked *lungi*s (a type of sarong in South Asia worn only by men) with white *tupi*s (a rounded skullcap often worn for prayer) on their heads making their way to the makeshift mosques. Unlike other evenings, no football match was scheduled to air that night, and thus roadside restaurants stored away their antique televisions as the tables became unoccupied. Women retreated indoors from the doorsteps of their modest dwellings, and only a handful of shelters showed any signs of light – the flickering of a candle, a *hariken* (kerosene lamp), or for the very lucky few, a single bulb lighted by solar panels.

At the end of a bend, we climbed up a steep flight of doughy clay steps, taking care not to trip and fall in the darkness – the earth still damp from the flashes of heavy rain that often come and go during the summer monsoon season. Standing outside her shelter, holding a *hariken*, and waiting to receive us was 27-year-old Rahima. The bags under her eyes and the deep cut mark on her right cheek revealed the signs of a young woman affected by a deeply profound tragedy. As we embraced, we cried together.

We entered Rahima's one-room shelter; the burning light of the *hariken* was just enough for us to see each other as we sat around it on straw mats pulled over the dusty floor. The room was mostly bare, save for a few belongings and some cookware piled together at the back of the shelter. A thin string was tied to the bamboo walls along the width of the room – the hanging, flimsy pink cloth now undrawn. 'The curtain makes me feel like I have two rooms and some privacy. It gives me a sense of safety. I have to keep my children safe. I am only living for them now,' Rahima would later tell me. Rahima's four-year-old daughter sat close by, holding on to the end of her mother's shawl; her two sons, aged ten and eight, crouched in the corner, looking on quietly. Rahima held my hands the entire time as she recounted her horrific and heartbreaking journey of fleeing to Bangladesh with her three children. She has not been able to see or speak to her husband, Ashraf, since she fled to Cox's Bazaar just a few days earlier. Ashraf remains jailed in Myanmar, though she's not entirely sure why, other than simply for being Rohingya. Rahima, Munni, and I spoke for hours. Life in the camps has been bleak and difficult, but Rahima has been finding moments of hope. At one point, she said quietly:

> I feel like we are just floating through this life. [*silence for a few minutes; she is crying now*] *Ya Allah!* It seems we will only keep floating until the day we die.

Rahima's metaphor of 'floating through life' was haunting – I had to jot it down in my notebook. She said the last few words almost in a whisper, and I could barely hear her when she immediately began sobbing. At this point she was inconsolable, and she held me tightly, placing her forehead on our interlocked hands, the tears continuously streaming down. She did not say a word. We sat in silence for more than an hour and cried together.

As Munni, Zia, Absar, and I drove away from Balukhali in the dead of the night, long after Isha (the night prayer) had ended, the peacefulness in the air was interrupted by the distant sounds of loud cries coming from the camps. 'What is that sound, Zia?' I asked my friend. 'Every day late at night, the refugees will cry as they remember their nearest and dearest,' Zia told me. 'They cry for the loved ones they lost, and pray for comfort and peace for their souls.' I thought of Rahima and prayed that she could find relief.

1

Introduction

Until 2017, Rohingyas – often dubbed the 'most persecuted minority in the world' – making the perilous trek across the border into Bangladesh were predominantly male, as they were not only denied citizenship and legal rights in Myanmar, but they also lacked economic opportunities within the country to support their families and communities (Kojima 2015; Albert 2017). On 25 August 2017, an escalation of violence in Rakhine State in Myanmar – where the Rohingyas largely resided – reached a tipping point, with horrific reports of murder and kidnapping of Rohingya men by Burmese soldiers, forced public nudity and humiliation, and sexual slavery and gang rape by military captivity directed against Rohingya women and girls. These attacks resulted in a humanitarian disaster that forced over 700,000 Rohingyas to flee their native land and seek refuge in the makeshift and overpopulated refugee camps outside of Cox's Bazaar, Bangladesh – specifically the Kutupalong–Balukhali mega-camp (used interchangeably with 'camp' or 'camps' throughout this book) – making it the largest refugee crisis in the world. Compared with past waves of refugees, there was a drastic increase in the number of women and girls crossing the border into Bangladesh. The concentration of refugees in Bangladesh's refugee camps is amongst the densest in the world, with tarpaulin and bamboo shelters precariously built on sharply sloped hillsides. There are now an estimated over 1 million Rohingya refugees living in the overcrowded and squalid camps, as the influx continued steadily over the subsequent months, with the majority of the camp's residents being women and girls (Ellis-Petersen 2019).

Unlike most debates on forced migration which focus on the larger structural needs of refugees, this book focuses on the lived experiences of Rohingya refugee women. Discussions of power relations and the reproduction of power asymmetries are often neglected in the dominant literature on refugee women's everyday subjectivities. The narratives of Rohingya women's perception of their own lives and the ways in which they negotiate, navigate, contest, and adjust to their surroundings are vital for understanding how these women forge kinship networks and learn to *make a life* in their new surroundings. The effects of forced migration on subjectivity are profound – understanding the lived experiences of women and their narratives of change can yield important insights into refugee women's notions about their self, their community, and their gendered bodies.

Answering these questions required 14 months of feminist ethnographic research, conducted between 2017 and 2018 (as well as frequent return to the camps every few months over the course of two years between 2018 and 2020) in the Rohingya refugee camps outside of Cox's Bazaar, Bangladesh. I examined the everyday negotiations, contestations, strategies, and coping mechanisms that Rohingya women use to affirm spaces for themselves. Refugee women are often assumed to be apolitical, disempowered, and non-agentic victims – vulnerable and dependent on men. Recognizing that they can simultaneously be victimized while remaining active agents of change in their lives provides a clearer understanding of their lives as refugees. Rohingya women do not fit neatly into monolithic discourses that portray them as lacking agency and unable to understand their predicament. Rather, despite their lives being marked by trauma and constraints, this book suggests that through everyday politics, Rohingya refugee women subvert, challenge, and negotiate patriarchal structures and power asymmetries, though in many ways they still affirm, bargain, and work *within* these structures. Strategic choices and bargaining are used to reach aspirations, reclaim identity and agency, and rebuild their lives, and their everyday tactics, creativity, and contestations challenge and overturn deeply embedded gender ideologies regarding women's place in settings after forced migration.

This book further reveals that the exercise of creating a sense of home and belonging after forced migration depends largely on individual experiences during displacement and the specific ways in which refugees *make a life* for themselves through economic, social, and cultural capital. Refugee women possess the creative capacity to employ frameworks of social organization created by themselves, which often deviate from the solutions offered by humanitarian aid agencies. They possess the capacity to bring about changes in their own lives through the various coping mechanisms they employ; the empowering spaces they create, inhabit, and reshape; and the bonds of kinship and community they forge.

Simon Turner (1999: 5) suggests that while gender identities and relations are not the only aspects of refugee life that are being transformed and challenged, 'gender appears to be the perspective through which most refugees attempt to understand social change'. Thus, I focus my ethnographic lens on the processes, relationships, and categories that illuminate the complexity of displacement, and the re-imagining of home, self, family, and identity in conflict-affected communities. My insights into these processes emerged from regular conversations with Rohingya women and others associated with the refugee camps. The women I met and spent months with spoke of their lives in Myanmar, where they were forced to live in 'modern-day concentration camps', the dangerous rickety boat journeys they took across the border, and their new lives in the overcrowded makeshift refugee camps in Bangladesh (Albert 2017). In documenting the effects of displacement, I found that Rohingya refugee women were yearning to have their stories, experiences, and emotions documented so that they could be shared with a wider audience, as they were acutely aware that their situation remains largely invisible to the rest of the world. For these women, the documenting of stories fulfils the crucial and urgent role of providing a voice to the forgotten victims of an emerging global crisis, thereby preserving historical memory for future generations (Abusharaf 2009). This book is hopefully a step forward in giving a voice to these women by following their narratives, words, and silences, with the hopes of enriching our understanding of how refugee women make a new life for themselves in refugee camps following expulsion from their native lands.

Gender, Forced Migration, Identities, and Lived Experiences

Positioned within a feminist ethnographic lens, this book addresses the effects of displacement and forced migration on women's lives and the transformations of gender roles and identities within a refugee camp by reflecting on their selfhood and subjectivity. It exposes the ways in which authority and power are constructed in refugee camps and affect women's social position within a community. Feminist ethnographers (Hackett 1996; Abusharaf 2009; McNamara 2009) have brought attention to the need to focus on the impact of forced migration on women and the importance of participatory research that uncovers their voices and viewpoints. In her comprehensive research on the situation of women refugees globally and how they differ from men, Jane Freedman (2007: 17) succinctly writes:

> …'what gender looks like' is not just about women, although women may be the primary subjects of much research on gender because it is they who suffer the primary consequences of gendered inequalities of power.

Thus, gendering forced migration entails 'making the invisible visible, bringing the margin to the center, rendering the trivial important, putting the spotlight on women as competent actors, understanding women as subjects in their own right rather than objects for men' (Reinharz 1992: 248).

A nuanced understanding of gender is crucial for comprehending the issues that affect the lives of Rohingya refugee women within the context of forced migration, their exercise of agency, as well as their modes of negotiating and navigating their gender identity in their everyday lives. I focus on the construction of gender as understood through its social practice, in the everyday experiences, negotiations, and navigations of gender identities in the marriage process, household relations, and encounters with NGOs and other refugees.

Emphasizing issues related to gender identities and roles in the refugee context is particularly important, as gender is the site 'where many negotiations and changes occur as a consequence of displacement' (Edward 2007: 5). Gender is considered to be a 'social construct' – that is, men and women carry out their daily practices in a manner that is strongly influenced by the 'social order' and societal culture (Kandiyoti 1988; Lorber 1994; Butler 1998; Ferree, Lorber, and Hess 1999). According to Judith Butler (1998), gender identities are the 'effects of signifying practices rooted in regimes of power-knowledge characterized as compulsory heterosexuality and phallocentrism' where men are placed at the centre of understandings of gender (Jagger 2008: 17). Thus, gender does not automatically impute any intrinsic qualities. Simone de Beauvoir (1988 [1953]: 295) argues that 'one is not born, but rather becomes, a woman' (also see Butler 1998). This captures succinctly the role society plays in establishing what it means to be a 'feminine' woman (or a 'masculine' man) and the way it creates distinct sexual binaries within a cultural context (Butler 1998: 29; Schrijvers 1999).

As this book highlights, understanding gender 'norms' and 'behaviours' requires unearthing the power structures and normative frames that are embedded within people's lives (Butler 1998: 29). The subtle, and often invisible, dynamics of power and status within a relation exist in a specific context that people are socialized to see as natural and inevitable. This is particularly the case for the Rohingya community, where the male–female binary is socially constructed and maintained based on culture and religion. What emerges through my research, however, is that these dominant frameworks of power and gender norms are negotiated, contested, and sometimes resisted by Rohingya women.

Candace West and Don H. Zimmerman (1987: 135) further argue that individuals are 'doing gender' continuously in their daily interactions, becoming 'accountable' for the performances they make. These interactions are shaped by social situations, as 'doing gender consists of managing such [social] occasions so that, whatever the particulars, the outcome is seen in context as gender-appropriate or ... gender-inappropriate, that is, *accountable*' (West and Zimmerman 1987: 135). In this way, society constitutes gender relations, as, according to Lucia McSpadden and Helene Moussa (1993: 204), gender allows for societies to 'construct ideas and knowledge about men and women' by allocating both sexes differing yet specified roles. Unequal power hierarchies arise from such notions of gender-appropriateness, which feminist scholars (Flax 1990; McSpadden and Moussa 1993; Indra 1998; Fiddian-Qasmiyeh 2014) have theorized as revealing the structural hierarchies, privileges, and relations of domination within and across gender.

Understanding gender thus requires studying the ways in which societal and cultural norms and practices shape the way people perceive concepts such as masculinity and femininity, male and female, and, more generally, 'how these notions structure human societies' (Indra 1998: 6). Societal and cultural norms play a disciplinary role by delineating the 'appropriate' behaviour of expected roles of men and women, which is particularly evident in the Rohingya community due to strict notions of 'manhood' and 'womanhood' (West and Zimmerman 1987). Thus, as Freedman (2007: 17) asserts, 'gendered meanings and roles are constructed and maintained, but also [negotiated,] contested' and redefined by men and women.

Studying the transformation of gender identities and changing gender relations among refugees forces us to think about gender roles, power relations, and identity construction. In this book, I look specifically at the marriage process, the gendered divisions of labour within the family, the gendered hierarchies of different individuals in the refugee camps, and the gendered effects of development programming. Pierrette Hondagneu-Sotelo (2000: 116) contends that 'we now have a clear understanding that migration is gendered and the gender relations change with migration processes'. To echo this, Elena Fiddian-Qasmiyeh (2014: 395) also notes that the role of gender in forced migration is key to understanding 'the different ways in which gender identities, roles, and relations are influenced by processes of and responses to forced migration'. The changing nature of these roles derives from entire social fabrics being uprooted and destroyed, the breakdown of former support structures, new and unfamiliar living environments that cause restricted mobility for both men and women, and entering new social relationships which may challenge old kinship structures. A gender-based approach thus serves to 'empower refugee women and their advocates' through an understanding of the gender relations that encompass refugee experiences (Giles, Moussa, and Esterik 1996, quoted in Edward 2007: 44; El Jack 2003: 3).

This gendered dimension of social relations, as Diane Elson (1996: 1) suggests, '[structures] the lives of individual women and men – such as the gendered division of labour and of access to and control over resources'. Displacement thus has 'profound effects on the gendered distribution of labour, on the way gendered relationships like marriage or parentage are organized, and on how gendered and other social roles change in terms of the obligations and rights these imply' (Lubkemann 2002: 5). At the household level, power relations and negotiations take place where men and women have specific roles and responsibilities 'expected' of them.

Alice Szczepaniková (2006: 1) suggests that 'migration is both a gendered and gendering process'. Differentiating between 'gendering' the analysis and the 'gendered' process is important for understanding the different dynamics at work within the same social space. To understand the gendered aspect of forced migration is to analyse the way migration is experienced differently by men and women – particularly in terms of the shift in relations between them as well as the dynamics of changing power differentials in these relationships. These changes cause gendered identities to be reconstructed and renegotiated during forced migration 'at the level of individual decisions and strategies embedded within family and wider social networks' (Szczepaniková 2006: 5). An example of this is the possibility of increased women's employment (as opposed to men's employment) in displacement, which results in a shift in gender relations and power dynamics within a household. Judy El-Bushra (2000), in her research on conflict in Rwanda, Somalia, and Uganda, argues that shifts in gender divisions of labour have created new opportunities for women as spaces open up for greater decision-making power within the family. Similarly, Jennifer Hyndman and Malathi de Alwis (2003) suggest that moving away from conservative 'masculine' and 'feminine' roles has caused women in Sri Lanka to assume new roles within their households and communities, such as partaking in income-generating activities.

Changing gender identities as a result of conflict and forced migration for both men and women can also, in some cases, result in gender-based violence. Traditional notions of masculinity and femininity related to 'appropriate' gender roles and relations in certain cultural contexts often transform or shift during times of conflict, but the way they affect gender-based violence in displacement is not always understood (Meertens and Segura-Escobar 1997;

Sideris 2003; Merry 2009). As family dynamics begin to change, erosion of male power and privilege at the socio-economic level, such as through loss of economic opportunities, unemployment, and men's inability to 'reconstruct' their position within the boundaries of the family, can have consequences resulting in gender-specific violence (Huseby-Darvas 1994; Colson 2003). Displacement thus provides a space for gender identities to be negotiated within marriage and the household – sometimes opening up new possibilities for 'empowerment', while at other times exposing them to various vulnerabilities.

A further aim of this book is to understand how Rohingya women negotiate their gendered identity after forced migration within the refugee camps in Bangladesh. Selfhood and subjectivity are integral to understanding the ways in which women renegotiate their gender identity. Tania Kaiser (2016: 198) succinctly notes 'how gender identities are constructed, understood, and interpreted, and how these processes relate to other aspects of their life and experience are also influential'. It is thus 'a social process individuals come to identify themselves with [that is] a particular configuration of social roles and relationships' (Grabska 2010: 33) where femininity and masculinity are based on particular expectations of how women and men should act. These may be norms, values, or behavioural patterns. For Rohingya women, identity emerges from the negotiation of 'expected' gender responsibilities and reproductive roles within the prevailing power structures of society. In this book, I ask how these gender identities – these specific femininities and masculinities – become transformed within the context of forced migration.

Examining women's gendered identities and how they are constructed in everyday life can provide a deeper understanding of Rohingya women's various negotiations and contestations within existing power relations in the refugee camps. Scholars such as Beatrice Hackett (1996), Ewa Morawska (2000), and Rogaia Abusharaf (2009) have written compelling ethnographies that explore the implications of forced migration and displacement on the formation – and transformation – of selfhood and subjectivity. It is in the context of profound war and violence that a 'creative shaping' of notions of self and society takes place to illuminate the ways in which women enact their gender identity, which is what Peter W. Preston (1997: 53) describes as an identity 'viewed as the outcome of complex social processes which embed the person in a series of social contexts'. Thus, to understand the experiences of refugee women, the analytical point of departure should focus on the ways that the gender identity of refugees affects how they 'construct and are exposed to danger', react and respond to multiple forms of violence and political uncertainty, and engage in forms of visibility and mobility in exile (Kaiser 2016: 197). It is in this manner that forced migration and displacement often lead to drastic and profound changes that transform every aspect of one's life – both public dimensions and intimate ones – dimensions such as 'feelings, strategies of self-representation and social interaction, and ability to imagine and create [refugees'] own life paths' (Nolin 2006; La Barbera 2015: 5).

Understanding subjectivities through a gendered analysis of forced migration helps to unravel the 'multiple pressures' and disparate opportunities that take place in the context of conflict, flight, and exile (Indra 1998; Fiddian-Qasmiyeh 2014; Kaiser 2016). These gendered identities and the way refugees begin to understand notions of self – and subsequently the creation of 'new selves' – are constantly renegotiated and reconstituted in migration and movement. It is what Aihwa Ong (1995: 350) describes as 'dwelling in traveling', since displacement, loss, and healing cause the forging of new identities and '[necessitate] the reconfiguration of selves and of relationships with others' (Abusharaf 2009: 10). What happens through the process of change and negotiation is that the self 'is always on the move' (Erchak 1992: 3; Abusharaf 2009).

Without erasing the distinct variations in refugee women's responses to their circumstances, understanding the re-creation of family and kinship ties, the establishment of new social networks, and the adoption of new cultural markers helps to reveal how women assume ownership of their gendered selves and recognize their agency (Abusharaf 2009; Fiddian-Qasmiyeh 2014). This narrative of agency and empowerment is ignored in many studies that talk about the 'refugee woman', as women are often portrayed as victims of war, dependent on men, and apolitical. In the literature on forced migration, the depiction of 'refugee women' as 'madonnalike' figures or weak victims without agency fails to recognize their multiple 'strategies of selfhood' for survival (Enloe 1991; Bhabha 1994; Malkki 1995; Chatty 2014; Fiddian-Qasmiyeh 2014). At the same time, agency must be contextualized in a new environment marked by different – and changing – societal constraints, gender differentials, and power hierarchies.

In her work with refugee women, Roberta Julian (1997) notes that refugee women are rarely consulted or given the opportunity to represent themselves in public forums to share their personal experiences; rather, they are spoken about and represented by others who ultimately portray a stereotypical image of them as 'victims'. This 'process of "victimization"', Julian (1997) suggests, controls the image of the refugee woman in larger public and political narratives of forced migration. Elena Fiddian-Qasmiyeh (2014: 398) further argues that before reducing refugee women's experiences to simply being vulnerable victims of sexual violence, it is important to recognize that 'displaced women could simultaneously be victim*ized* and yet remain active agents deserving of respect and not simply pity'. Patricia Daley (1991) takes the conversation a step further by suggesting that in many ways forced migration can be a 'liberating force' that helps women escape patriarchal control and find ways to challenge, negotiate, or even reinforce their expected gendered roles and behaviours. Katarzyna Grabska (2010), however, notes that while there may be liberatory aspects to refugee women's access to income and change in gender roles within the household, this 'does not necessarily lead to greater empowerment'.

Even in the most difficult of circumstances, women retain their agency and do not engage as mere 'passive bystanders' of power and domination; rather, they actively work to 'maximize their own life chances' through what Deniz Kandiyoti (1988: 280) considers the 'patriarchal bargain'. Narratives of Rohingya refugee women, their lived experiences, and the ways in which they negotiate, navigate, contest, and adjust to their new surroundings reveal that strategic choices and coping mechanisms are used to reach aspirations, reclaim identity and agency, and rebuild their lives.

A key assertion of this book is that Rohingya refugee women perform acts of resistance through their *everyday* actions. In thinking about women's agency, Amani El Jack (2008: 257) succinctly asserts that the transformation of gender roles and subjectivities in refugee contexts does 'not mean the end of patriarchy but rather the everyday practice of resistance and agency performed' by refugees. The acts of resistance performed by Rohingya women can be noted in the subtleties of everyday life. As Chandra Talpade Mohanty (2003: 83) writes, '… resistance inheres in the very gaps, fissures, and silences of hegemonic narratives…. Agency is thus figured in the small, day-to-day practices and struggles of Third World women.' Within the development studies discourse, the social transformation of gender dynamics has often been linked to notions of progress, with change (in social behaviour, norms, practices, and so on) presumed to be a linear process moving towards an idealized goal and normally associated with outward, public, and often vocal displays of 'resistance' (Crisol 2001). However, I argue that *incremental change*, or 'silent challenges' (El-Bushra 2000; Kabeer 2005), and everyday contestations against patriarchal oppression are often ignored when discussing transformation. Though these silent acts and performances may seem insignificant, they underscore how voice and public resistance are not the only forms of 'empowerment' and paths towards an idealized 'gender transformation' (Pedersen 2016). Rather, quotidian performances of resistance, negotiations, and contestations can bring about incremental changes – even if slow and undetectable – that translate into new patterns of living and forms of empowerment, both individually and collectively. In this manner, I suggest that Rohingya refugee women's *everyday*, small, mundane negotiations – which include women coming to terms with their new breadwinner role due to their husbands' lack of employment and husbands dealing with the loss of this 'traditional masculine' role – are a form of transformation in their own right. Culturally, these tensions, negotiations, and navigations underscore how transformation is not necessarily linear or openly broadcasted and cannot be measured against a particular set of economic or political baselines (Kabeer 2005). Rather, in many ways, it is a personal act of committing to change within given societal circumstances that by no means suggests an 'end to patriarchy' but rather a move towards 'disrupting and challenging the prevailing discourses of the powerful while providing space for solace, sharing, and collective empowerment' (Parpart 2010: 8).

Conceptualizing the Refugee Camp: Beyond 'Bare Life'

Living in a refugee camp is widely perceived to 'break down' and 'erode' traditional life, where 'refugees invariably live in conditions of insecurity and deprivation' that are 'harsh, dangerous and characterized by social chaos and lack of normal social structures' (Wilde 1998: 109–110; Bartolomei, Pittaway, and Pittaway 2003: 87). Giorgio Agamben (1998: 139) suggests that camps strip persons of identity and agency, essentially reducing them to 'bare life'. The camp, according to Agamben (1998: 139), is in a 'state of exception' where the rule of law does not hold and where 'life ceases to be politically relevant … and can as such be eliminated without punishment'. In the context of the Rohingya refugee camps, the Bangladeshi government considers Rohingya refugees to be 'extra-territorial *persona non-grata* and a threat to the country; therefore, they are placed within restricted boundaries controlled by specially designed rules and restrictions until official measures are taken for their repatriation' (Farzana 2015: 151). In embracing the 'refugee' label, Agamben (1998) contends that refugees must necessarily be helpless, dependent victims, essentially rendered a 'speechless emissary' (Malkki 1995). This, however, fails to take into account the materiality and heterogeneity of the social world of refugee camps and the diverse ways in which refugees themselves contribute to camps, transforming them into vibrant social spaces over time.

Agier (2014: 19, quoted in Turner 2015) further suggests that 'the camps are places of relative closure but they are also cosmopolitan cross-roads'. While insecurity and vulnerability drive people to refugee camps, insecurity alone does not entail the full extent of their experience and the simplicity of everyday life. Turner (2015: 143) argues that these spaces are filled with social life, where diverse norms and ideas work to 'create new identities'. In a similar vein, Julie Peteet (2005), through her own research of camps in the occupied Palestinian territories, suggests that studies of refugee camps must go beyond abstract, grand theories of 'bare life', but rather must be grounded 'empirically'.

Refugees in camps are thus not simply helpless victims; rather, they learn to adapt to the life of the camp. Adaptation to life in the camps may also cause 'new social forms and opportunities' to emerge, where *everyday life* is viewed through the mundane, daily routines of the *ordinary*) – where new identities materialize and social worlds are transformed, making life in the camp different from life elsewhere (Turner 2004; Peteet 2005; Gren 2015).

Refugee camps are shaped by ambivalence and contradictions – they are neither 'neutral' spaces of humanitarianism nor perfect 'safe harbours' for refugees (Turner 2015). Rather, it is an 'out-of-the-way place' – to borrow from Anna Tsing (1993) – where new social imaginaries, expanded possibilities, and the transformations of 'being and becoming' someone take place (Turner 2015). Refugee camps are thus carefully constructed spaces in which women, men, girls, and boys attempt to *make a life* – a life that is meaningful and hopeful despite the various adversities and constraints that they face. Time and locale within the camp are 'made meaningful, albeit within the spatial and temporal peculiarities of the camp' (Turner 2015: 143).

Any analysis about camps and refugees must be integrated using a feminist theoretical lens and from a gendered perspective. The refugee camp, instead of being a space of 'exception', is instead a microcosm of a larger system of power intertwined with gender, race, and class, as well as other systems of social inequality and subjugation. The whole process of forced migration and displacement is a gendered process, and gender identities, roles, and relations can be challenged and negotiated in the process of migration. Refugee camps thus provide an opportunity to transform the structures of domination and power. I agree further with Turner (1999, 2004) who, in his study of a Tanzanian refugee camp, finds that social changes and transformation are primarily perceived through the prism of gender. Furthermore, Asha Hans (2012) suggests that focusing on camp contexts emerged from the gendered experiences of subaltern women, which have occupied a central position within risk zones, and that central to a woman's experiences is her body and her sex. Women remain in a precarious position during the process of displacement as they must deal with the new challenges of refuge. In adjusting to their new circumstances, they remain resilient, transforming the refugee camps in a way that contests deeply held gender structures.

Through the everyday lives and lived experiences of Rohingya refugee women, as this book shows, there is more to refugees than *bare life*; instead, refugees cope with the hardships and conditions of exile and express social and economic agency even in the most difficult circumstances. The camp creates a space where Rohingya women's gender identities and subjectivities and their gender and social relations are transformed, negotiated, and contested.

Overview of the Book

This book is divided into eight chapters that weave together an ethnography that *tells stories* and *unfolds lives*. In the next chapter, Chapter 2, I discuss the methodological frameworks that form the foundation of this research. I introduce my ethnographic field site and the spaces I inhabited, the women's worlds I entered, and the constraints attached to conducting ethnographic fieldwork in these spaces. This is followed by Chapter 3, which situates the recent migration of Rohingyas from Myanmar to Bangladesh within the greater context of conflict, systemic violence, and oppression in Myanmar's recent history. This chapter introduces the Rohingya as a borderland people in Myanmar, their life under siege, and provides a glimpse into Rohingya gender relations and roles prior to displacement.

To elucidate the narratives of the everyday, in Chapters 4–7, I explore the subtle ways in which women seek to *make a life* in their new host communities by providing thick descriptions and ethnographies. These chapters demonstrate that refugee life within the Kutupalong–Balukhali mega-camp in Bangladesh shapes their gendered identities in distinct ways.

Chapter 4 examines the experience of home and belonging after Rohingya women arrived at the camps. I illustrate the re-establishment of life after migration, where bonding, kinship, and social organization are of utmost importance. This chapter engages with Rohingya women's profound, productive actions as they craft a sense of 'home', 'place', and belonging and, in the process, negotiate their gendered identities and subjectivities. I further explore the desire for social continuity in the formation of community and the way social relations and practices shape the physical and social environment to 'impose symbolic meaning on place' (Peteet 2005). In particular, I show how placemaking through spaces such as the *taleem* provides moments of respite during hardship through collective prayer and creates a sense of belonging and semblance of 'home' in displacement.

In Chapter 5, using the voices of young Rohingya women, I explore some of the aspects of the marriage process that colour everyday life in the camps, as the negotiation of gender identities and practices through marriage and family expectations is a particular part of the encampment process. Marriage is fundamental to life in the camps – it recreates the bonds of family that may have been lost or damaged during migration. Contestations around gender identities are part of the refugee experience, and the negotiations of norms through marriage, marriage processes, and family life are examples of this.

Chapter 6 delves into the various bargaining strategies and power asymmetries through the politics of housework, paid work, and familial or gendered responsibilities and duties within marriage and the household. This chapter illustrates that changing gender relations are related to negotiations and transformations taking place within the household. It captures the changing gender relational dynamics after displacement with regard to work and livelihoods and their effects on gender subjectivity, suggesting that displacement has created not only a crisis of masculinity but also a crisis of femininity.

The preceding chapters revealed gender dynamics regarding marriage and the household and the factors that shape Rohingya women's agency, negotiations, and navigations in these spheres. However, these changing dynamics must also be gauged alongside the new currents of change brought about by the burgeoning humanitarian aid agencies that have mushroomed across the camps. The final ethnography chapter, Chapter 7, extends debates on gender and humanitarian aid and analyses Rohingya women's encounters with, and exposure to, the humanitarian or NGO industry as well as 'gender programming', and how these programmes directly impact and transform gender asymmetries within the camps.

Taken together, Chapters 4–7 offer a unique perspective, weaving together an intricate narrative of transforming gender relations and roles and the negotiation of identities and relationships among Rohingya women in Bangladesh's refugee camps. These chapters illuminate Rohingya women's voices and viewpoints and the powerful and often vibrant relationships that unfold in settings of despair and struggle through the friendships, social networks, and explorations of self and community that take place. In the final chapter, Chapter 8, I conclude with an overview of the book's contributions to knowledge and what prospects remain for the future of Rohingya refugees – particularly Rohingya women.

2

Stories and Silences
On Entering and Writing Women's Worlds

A Town Transformed

When I began fieldwork in August 2017 in Cox's Bazaar, Bangladesh, it was not my first trip to the seaside town. I had visited Cox's Bazaar several times over the years, particularly during my childhood on trips to Bangladesh to visit relatives, and I remembered it always having the same rush of tourists flocking the city centre bazaars, with bicycle rickshaws and CNGs (auto-rickshaws) caught in stifling traffic jams and the sounds of holidaymakers partying through the night. In late 2016 and early 2017, I visited the Rohingya refugee camps (located 20 miles outside of Cox's Bazaar town) for the first time as part of a humanitarian project I was helping to organize. At that time, the camps consisted of a small number of refugees – a few thousand – who had fled to Bangladesh from Myanmar at varying periods over the past three decades. Only a handful of humanitarian organizations had set up shop in the centre of town. Nobody had anticipated a sudden influx of over a million people in the months to come.

When I returned to Bangladesh eight months later, in August of that year, the ambience felt starkly different. On the flight from Dhaka to Cox's Bazaar, it was unsettling to find myself as one of the only people of Bangladeshi heritage on a flight that was usually always filled with locals heading to a weekend getaway. This time, the flight was filled with international UN aid workers, NGO staff, and government officials. Driving into Cox's Bazaar from the airport was an even greater shock. Bangladeshi tourists were few and far between, and the streets were now filled with foreigners and humanitarian aid staff eager to 'see' firsthand the effects of the recent influx of Rohingyas from Myanmar. I was now one of them. The realization that I too had become a part of this sudden 'fascination' with the plight of the Rohingyas, and what that means for the ways we use the marginalized to obtain 'breaking news', would trouble me throughout my fieldwork and to this day.

When I had planned to conduct research on the Rohingya refugee situation in the middle of the first year of my PhD in early 2017, I could never have anticipated that my fieldwork would coincide with the mass exodus of over a million Rohingyas. At the start of my PhD, I envisioned a very different type of project – one that was based on my earlier experiences in the refugee camps – much smaller at the time, where I led several humanitarian relief projects. But when I later 'entered' the field in August 2017, all the questions, assumptions, and plans I had so meticulously prepared as an eager PhD student were completely turned on their head. Only a few days after I arrived at the camps did the initial mass exodus commence. Bearing witness to the indescribable scenes of suffering and tragedy forced me to rethink everything and remove any illusions I had of what it means to be a researcher. But I was ready to learn – not from within the walls of the ivory tower, but from the hearts and minds of those who had experienced *life* more than me. I was the student, and the Rohingyas – my interlocutors – were my teachers.

Power, Knowledge, and Feminist Ethnography

Through feminist ethnography, I analyse the various gendered subjectivities and lived experiences of refugee women. In adopting a feminist ethnographic approach, I have placed the voices of my interlocutors at the centre of my analysis, which has also directly guided the writing process (Ong 1988; Abu-Lughod 1990; Mohanty 1991a). As a qualitative method of research, feminist ethnography offers detailed descriptions of daily life through the narratives of those who experience it firsthand (Behar and Gordon 1995). Feminist ethnography in cases of forced migration – as Rogaia Abusharaf (2009: 5) suggests in her work on South Sudanese displaced women – 'is an essential tool for narrating the experiences and perspectives of people living with the unspeakable consequences of mass atrocities'. For her, there is 'urgency' in defining how the experiences of displaced women as gendered bodies have been widely ignored from discussions on conflict and forced migration. This framework guided the ethics of my fieldwork process by interrogating the power of knowledge claims through the questions I asked my interlocutors, as well as the various silences and moments that were unspoken. This allowed me to pay attention to marginalized narratives that have been glossed over in discussions on forced migration. In order to understand gender relations and women's everyday lives after forced migration, a feminist methodology allowed me to understand the structures of relations of subordination and women's experiences within these oft-invisible structures of gender power.

This methodology was an essential tool for narrating the experiences and perspectives of Rohingya women by positioning my interlocutors' voices, narratives, and ordeals at the centre of the analysis.

Throughout this book, my focus as a feminist ethnographer has been to place a critical lens on gender that involves questioning common-sense assumptions about men and women, masculinity and femininity, and the details of the power dynamics at play. I worked to interrogate the power differentials and gendered nuances between my Rohingya male and female interlocutors, as well as the power differentials between myself as the researcher and my interlocutors. Reflexivity allowed me to constantly interrogate my own position as the researcher and my 'social location' in relation to my interlocutors, thus forcing me to question how my own background and experiences influenced the words of my interlocutors and the research that I produced (Reid, Greaves, and Kirby 2017). Even in discussions with my research assistants, Zia and Munni, I constantly reflected on the unique position they occupied as 'privileged insiders' who have unqualified access to a camp 'outsider', boosting their own personal status, and how this may have affected their interactions with refugees in the camp. Furthermore, as a feminist ethnography, this book critically analyses Rohingya women's lives beyond the restricted categories of 'victimhood' and 'agency' – or even 'emancipation' – and instead recognizes the everyday choices and negotiations Rohingya women make within the constraints of their physical and social environment. In representing and constructing the lives of my interlocutors, I have attempted to move beyond dichotomies such as 'victimhood' and 'agency' by recognizing that choice and constraint are intertwined in Rohingya women's everyday lives.

Feminist research takes pains to provide empathetic representation of people's experiences through a dialectical relation of listening and responding to interlocutors, and eventually telling their stories (Wolf 1996). The power of narrative methods in forced migration research cannot be understated as it brings out stories of *everyday life*, and 'how people themselves as "experiencing subjects" make sense of violence and turbulent change' (Eastmond 2007: 249). Eastmond's notion of 'stories' is an important tool to understand lived experience, as it lays bare the nuances of life not as hard 'truths' but as an 'interplay between life, experience and story'. Prior to commencing my fielding, I contemplated on the method of interviewing, conversations, and narratives. Some questions filled my mind: *How will I interview my interlocutors? What questions would be most appropriate? Should I take notes while listening? Should I have specific questions?* Once I became a part of women's life-worlds, I realized that asking specific questions seldom revealed the entirety of their experiences. There is meaning in listening, in being part of conversations where women engage in their everyday interactions, speaking in an open-ended manner, giving voice to the lives that are organically unfolding, they are vividly experiencing, and that are always in the making (Eastmond 2007). The retelling of an experience can be produced differently depending on the situation – whether in a formal setting, group interview, and so on. The most vivid sharing of narratives and 'stories' emerged in *everyday* settings with my interlocutors – conversations shared over tea, on the side of the dusty path as I walked from one shelter to another, during weddings, after prayer, on the way to fill a pot of water at the tube-well. This fluidity permitted my interlocutors to become active participants in the production of knowledge, thereby allowing 'previously occluded parts of women's experiences to be brought to light' (Parashar 2016: 44).

First-person narratives allow for retelling and interpreting experiences in a way that communicates women's everyday subjectivities. These subjectivities through 'stories' in feminist research reveal not another 'collection of tales of woe' but rather a deeper understanding of women as gendered beings who 'seek to make sense of displacement, re-establish identity in ruptured life courses and communities, or bear witness to violence and repression' (Eastmond 2007: 1). Narratives are powerful commentaries on the fashioning of women's gender identity in their everyday lives. As my interlocutors recounted their narratives, I took time to listen, understand, and empathize with their silences, blank stares, and the varying tones, degrees, and inflections of body language. I observed emotions, often experiencing it with them, and noted their intensities and variations. My interlocutors' responses also depended on the setting we were in, who was around, and how they felt.

As there are power asymmetries between the researcher and interlocutor, particularly when using the narrative method, I have tried my best to remain in continuous dialogue with my interlocutors and worked to ensure that I built trust and rapport with them, placing 'both the researched [my interlocutors] and the researcher [me] in a relationship of some intimacy' (McNamara 2009). When listening to my interlocutors' narratives of violence and oppression, it was important for me to engage them with empathy, understanding, friendship, and solidarity. And so many times we cried together – my interlocutors and I. We held each other as they shared difficult memories and stories of pain and suffering. In those moments I *listened* and *learned*, ultimately leading to what can be said to be an 'empathic and collaborative form of investigation' when conducting feminist research and writing a feminist ethnography (McNamara 2009).

Entering Women's Worlds

Part of the ethics of feminist research is to maintain a commitment to producing well-informed research by being self-reflexive and having an acute awareness of my positionality as a researcher and the ways in which my privileges shape my approach to conducting this research. My own identity cannot be abstracted from the context of my research, though in many ways, aspects of my identity helped me to build trust and rapport with my interlocutors as well as a long-term relationship with them. Successfully studying the intricacies of gender identities, subjectivities, and relations in the Rohingya community required access to women's spaces and their inner lives – the Rohingyas are a particularly conservative community, and thus it would only be feasible for a woman to enter these spaces and spend a significant period of time with Rohingya women.

Beyond simply being a woman, however, other aspects of my identity occupied multiple subject positions in my fieldwork. Like my interlocutors, there was a point of commonality – being a Muslim from a religiously conservative background who also wears the *hijab*. There were, of course, many differences – I am a Canadian of ethnic Bangladeshi descent. I would often oscillate between these identities – on the one hand, as an *insider* fitting neatly into the category of Muslim, dressing and looking very much like them and yet, on the other hand, still being an *outsider* as a Bangladeshi and a foreigner of a different social status, class, and educational level. I remember on my first day of fieldwork, one of my interlocutors, Zannat, told me: '*Afa*, you are like us. But you are also very lucky unlike us.' I must admit that this poignant admission affected me tremendously by forcing me to constantly negotiate how I was perceived by my interlocutors, the power differentials involved, and recognizing how much my multiple identities were interwoven in this research. This statement prompted me to rethink the epistemological implications of my own positionality and the biases that come into play (Hartsock 1983). Thinking through my 'relational positionality', which underscores my position as a researcher amongst my interlocutors, Zannat's statement forced me to consider how nationality, race, religion, language, and class were all intertwined in the way my interlocutors perceived me (Crossa 2012). Though I made every possible effort to share in their experiences as one of their peers, the reality was that I was an 'outsider' with many privileges that they did not have, even though many aspects of my identity gave me an 'insider' perspective. I may have been Muslim, from a traditional and conservative family background with similar cultural and religious values to the Rohingyas, but the reality was that I was a person of Bangladeshi heritage – a member of the dominant culture in the Rohingya's new country of refuge; I was also a foreigner – raised abroad in a middle-class family my whole life; I was a fluent English speaker; I had the luxury of movement – to enter and leave the refugee camps as I pleased. Thus, I agree with Veronica Crossa (2012: 115), who argues that 'relational positionality' – that is, the various identities of the researcher – 'are shaped by multiple mobile and flexible relations and how that makes a difference to the research process'. It is not necessarily the fact that I am a Bangladeshi, Western, Muslim, female student that affects my research but rather the way these aspects of my identity affected how my interlocutors negotiated their interactions and conversations with me. The power dynamics between me and my interlocutors thus always lurked in the shadows of my ongoing social interactions in the camps, and I tried consciously to steer attention away from my privileged subjectivities when probed by my interlocutors about various aspects of my life.

Over the course of my fieldwork, what became clear was that one of the most important factors that allowed me to build strong bonds of trust and friendships with my interlocutors was my willingness to *listen*, alongside my deliberate and conscious efforts to become a part of my interlocutors' life-worlds. Within a short time, I was called *afa* (a respectful and endearing term meaning 'big sister') by my interlocutors. I took great care to ensure that my interlocutors felt comfortable sharing with me their personal narratives and their inner lives. And in many ways, I was eager to learn from them and share spaces with them, and become a part of their life-worlds. During downtime and light-hearted conversations as we sat on mats and sang or danced together, my interlocutors and I shared similar personal stories of family background, love, and marriage. My family experiences and stories about my own marriage were a point of interest in many conversations, and these prolonged interactions often made our exchanges feel like that of close friends rather than researcher-interlocutor.

A number of scholars posit that female researchers may become 'genderless, androgens, or acquire a status of an honorary male' (Grabska 2010: 66). In many ways, this *insider–outsider* status also proved helpful as I interacted with Rohingya refugee men as well as Rohingya leaders and religious figures in the camp, as they often viewed me not only as a local but also as someone outside of the humanitarian aid industry without any political inclinations. It was thus possible for me to navigate the various social circles within the camp.

One day, one of my interlocutors, 28-year-old Sakina, said to me as we sat together at the *taleem* (gathering for prayer) after a long session of supplication, her eyes filled with tears:

> You are not like the others that come here. So many people just come here for a short time and write our difficult experiences down. They take our information and we never see them again. You are the only one here with us for many days and listening to our stories. Nobody is spending time with us like you. *Shukoriya* [thank you].

These words were a moving reminder that it was important to become a part of the life-worlds of my interlocutors – an active 'participant', rather than a mere 'observer', what Patricia Adler and Peter Adler (1994) call an 'active member-researcher'. As I attempted to find out about Rohingya women's *everyday* lives in the camps, I had to become part of their various activities throughout the day. These quotidian nuances necessitated a type of immersion that could not be found in merely asking questions through interviews. Rather, I became part of their rituals and routines. I spent time with them in their shelters; we cooked and chopped up vegetables together, sitting on the floor, sharing laughs; I participated in weddings, *taleems*, and *majhee* meetings. Through my attendance at food and sanitary pad distributions, NGO training workshops, and medical visits, I took notes and became a familiar face in the community, making friends and noting the moments of solitude, silence, and the sometimes mundane parts of everyday life in the camps.

And thus, I was able to *witness* numerous interactions and relationships unfolding, writing thorough fieldnotes on my reflections, thoughts, feelings, experiences, and my place in the lives of my interlocutors. In listening to my interlocutors' conversations, I noted down the silences and trivial aspects of everyday life, paid attention to the patterns of their activities, and *learned* the sorrow and raw emotion through the 'silent unspoken, not easily observable, but fundamentally real' (Hearn and Parker 2001: 12). As such, 'hanging out with refugees' and taking an interest in the life-worlds of my interlocutors with patience and personal interest, and being present and active when various events took place, was an important part of the ethnography (Rodgers 2004).

Feminist research prioritizes building relationships with refugees – thus, interviews should not be 'too fast, too purposive, or much too short'; rather, they must be open and allow interlocutors to take their time to respond, to discuss matters that are important to them without cutting them off, and to present their stories with the 'messy' nuances of unrushed language (Ghorashi 2008: 118). Thus, the importance of language and the quality of translation becomes even more pressing. One afternoon while I was writing down some quotes from my interlocutor Zannat, though she did not understand what I was writing, she noticed that I was translating each word individually and asking my research assistant Munni to double-check the meaning of each word. She suddenly lit up and told me that she was grateful that I was translating and writing down every single word: 'So many people come here and we talk to them. But they never write down our words in the way you're writing them down. If I say ten sentences they will summarize it into one.' I appreciated Zannat telling me this – it was an important reminder of the time and value that our interlocutors give us as researchers to share their stories and that their words must be respected and cannot – and *should not* – be simplified. For the most part, I attempted to keep translation from the Rohingya language to Bangla to English at a minimum, as translations between multiple languages could be tricky, and so I almost always ventured to take the original Rohingya and translate it directly into English. Representing the full 'story' required sticking to the original as much as possible without summarizing, simplifying, or generalizing it.

Leaving and Writing Women's Worlds

Though Sakina's words, 'Nobody is spending time with us like you', were a moving reminder of why long-term ethnographic research is important, like others, I too had to leave one day, and I was acutely aware and mindful of this reality. Throughout my fieldwork, however, I worked to constantly self-reflect on the power relationships that formed and my privileges as someone who could easily leave and move while my interlocutors could not, and it was this constant reflection that guided me during my writing process. Though my sustained, *everyday* relationships with my interlocutors had ended, I agree with feminist researchers who suggest that the nurturing of those relationships and the essence of fieldwork remain even long after the researcher has left the physical 'field' and linger on during the writing process. I continue – even to this day – to return to the camps every few months even after the initial 14 months of fieldwork, and through these visits and subsequent phone calls, messages, and video calls with my interlocutors in the camps, I have been in constant contact with them. Sometimes, these conversations involved further analysis of the data; other times, they revealed new information that had unfolded after my departure from the field. Thus, these genuine friendships that continued long after my time in the field have been integral to the way my interlocutors' voices have been unveiled throughout the pages of this book.

Fieldwork also left me with countless piles of notes, images, and videos – making sense of it all and attempting to encapsulate the extent of my conversations and interactions with my interlocutors was a daunting experience. All the interviews were transcribed and translated word for word to ensure that I had noted and included all of my interlocutors' non-verbal emotions, feelings, and actions to capture and enrich the essence of their experiences and the meaning of the spoken words. What followed was what Denzin (2009) calls 'the art of interpretation', requiring a deep process of coding the material, finding patterns, and creating themes that trace back to my interlocutors' experiences of gendered negotiations within the refugee camps as the main coding category. Theme-making, however, was not a linear process as I had to read and re-read my notes coupled with manual coding that emerged to identify the countless categories that would ultimately be narrowed down to what remains within these pages as 'the final tale of the field' (Van Maanen 2011).

A feminist ethnographic approach (Abu-Lughod 1990; Mohanty 1991b; Ong 1988) allowed me to position the participants' voices at the centre of the analysis throughout the writing process. The structure and presentation of the research are thus a 'thematic narrative' with the stories at the centre, followed by analytic and interpretive commentary (Emerson, Fretz, and Shaw 2011: 171). Emerson, Fretz, and Shaw (2011: 202) suggest that a thematic narrative is analytically thematized, but often in relatively loose ways, 'in order to build up a series of thematically organized units of excerpts and analytic commentary'. Thus, the narratives and excerpts that are used in this book go beyond simply illustrating an idea; rather, they are used as 'building blocks for constructing and telling [the] story' (Emerson, Fretz, and Shaw 2011: 171).

But the writing process was not easy – there were many nights where I cried for hours as I re-read the stories my interlocutors entrusted me with. I wept not only because of the horrific nature of the violence and trauma they faced but also over the impossibility of doing justice to the gravity of their words, narratives, *everyday lived experiences*. In every word that I wrote, I was reminded of my responsibility to share a story that was not mine – it was an obligation of trust since my interlocutors urged me to share their story with the world. An elderly interlocutor in her late sixties, Khatun Khalamma, told me one day in a very loving manner: 'You are now bearing witness to all of this suffering. On Qiyamat [Day of Judgement] Allah will ask us all – what have we done to help our brothers and sisters?' She was kind about it, trying not to directly question me, but I nonetheless understood the cultural nuances of such a question – as elders often share their wisdom with the youth in a roundabout sort of way in an effort to give advice – I knew it was meant to advise me. I have wrestled with this reminder every single day since. Though I have supported and will continue to be involved in the refugee camps even after my departure, the question of how this *research* – this *written document* – will help the Rohingyas has been a difficult one to answer. *Who is this research for? Whose aims is this serving? What actually is the purpose of all this?*

Thinking through ethics and the writing process also forced me to interrogate questions around power and privilege – particularly which voices to highlight and include and which ones to exclude. These choices were difficult. Long-term ethnographic research necessarily means we end up with a large stockpile of information, yet what remains within these pages are only a limited number of voices from the various I interacted with. Each bit of information left out is a piece of reality denied the light of day. Part of the writing process was ensuring that I was accurately depicting the voices of my interlocutors as they would have liked. I strived to ensure a truthful representation by sharing various versions of chapter drafts (by reading them aloud) with my interlocutors and soliciting their feedback, which is part of the beauty of long-term, sustained engagement with interlocutors – ensuring that I gave justice to their voices and experiences.

Similarly, a significant portion of the writing-up process entailed thinking through how to engage with and write about the horrific and unimaginable suffering of others. Much of the words and thoughts conveyed by my interlocutors were traumatic and emotional; thus, during writing up, I made a conscious effort to share the entirety of my interlocutors' experiences, including all the minute, raw details often neglected in traditional academic writing. Being present in the camps for several months assisted me in getting many details of their past suffering, as sometimes my interlocutors would share part of a painful story and only continue the story after several weeks. My efforts to authentically represent their words were facilitated by the fact that a lot of my interlocutors' communications were non-verbal – many conversations involved only a few words but were punctuated by long periods of very meaningful silence. A few words would be shared, and then perhaps 5–10 minutes of complete silence would pass as they held their faces in their hands, cried, shifted, or conveyed some other expression. I carefully documented all of the details of these *unsaid* moments – the length of silence, the topic being discussed, the number of people present, the intensity of the sobbing – which were important for providing vital context to the larger verbal narrative. As part of constructing a narrative of their thoughts and experiences, my focus as a researcher was on the voices *within* the narrative – the *said* as well as the *unsaid*. It was the *unsaid* moments that weaved together a clearer and more raw expression of their *said* expressions. Reading and understanding those unsaid expressions allowed me as the researcher to paint a larger portrait of my interlocutors' narratives, as simply conveying their spoken comments would severely misrepresent the complexities and nuances of their raw and authentic experiences.

Even as the writing process came to an end, I continued to struggle with these thoughts, but the words of Patricia McNamara (2009) were helpful in making sense of these feelings. She suggests that the value of writing a feminist ethnography must go beyond simply remaining within the purview of academic scholarship. Rather, storytelling must 'make a difference' – that is, it must work to make a strong impact in advancing the welfare of our interlocutors. And so, for me, I hope the words of my interlocutors are not left to gather dust within the pages of this book – that instead, they open up a means of understanding the lives of those who are so often forgotten.

Setting the Scene

The Road to Kutupalong–Balukhali

Each morning I sat in the car with my research assistants and friends, Munni and Zia, and driver Absar as we moved from our small guesthouse at the edge of the tourist town of Cox's Bazaar. We drove along the long road, past the waves of the Bay of Bengal and Cox's Bazaar Beach – the longest natural sea beach in the world – past dozens of cars, small minivans, and *tomtom*s zooming past us. The hour-long journey took us off the main road, where we turned left on an unmarked, potholed dirt path, past local Bangladeshi villages; the *ring-ring* sound of rickshaws and laughter of Bangladeshi children running after cars is noticeable as we drove past. We passed luscious green rice fields and forest trees on long and winding roads for a little over an hour before coming upon a large expanse of sandy, rugged hills. As we drew closer to the entrance of the camp, large groups of local Bangladeshis from surrounding villages set up shops selling all kinds of items – fruit, vegetables, tarpaulin, and so on – and the roads were adorned with pro-refugee banners hanging between trees. Upon getting closer to the camps, a large sign written on a concrete edifice towards the camp said: 'No Access without Permission' in Bangla. The Bangladeshi military monitored who could or could not enter the camp. They stopped our car, asking me and Zia what business we had in the place before letting us go through. We snaked through the narrow, dusty road of the makeshift camp before parking in the middle of the main bazaar (Figures 2.1–2.2).

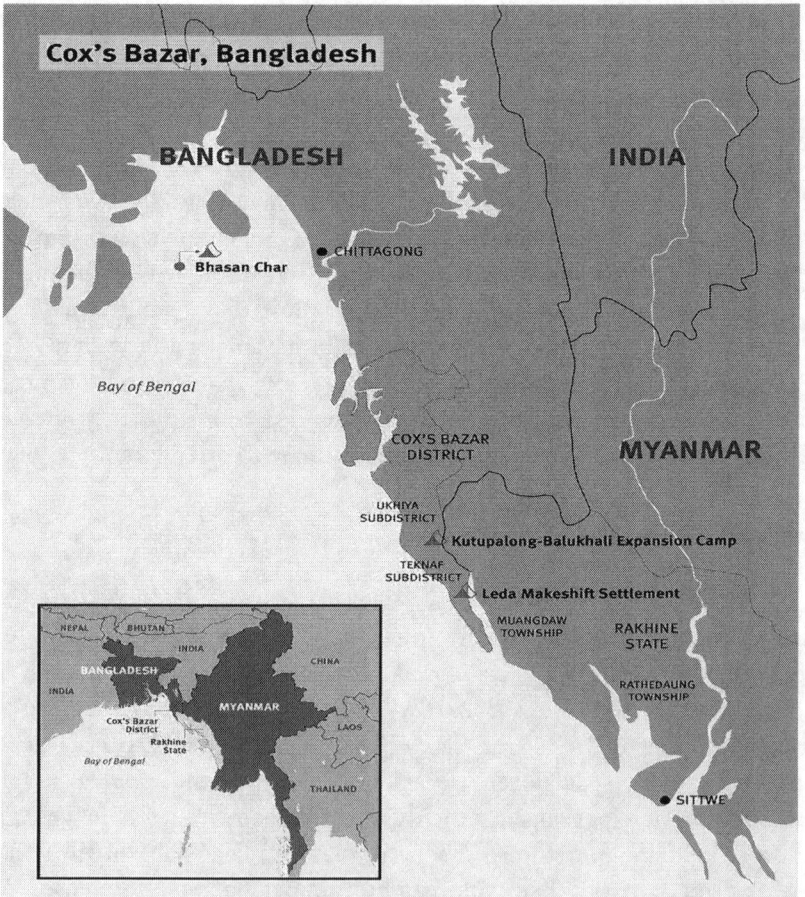

Figure 2.1 Location of the Rohingya refugee camps

Source: © 2018 Human Rights Watch.

Note: Map not to scale and does not represent authentic international boundaries.

Figure 2.2 A small section of the Kutupalong–Balukhali mega-camp in Bangladesh (December 2017)

Source: Photo by author.

Features of the Mega-Camp

Located in southeastern Bangladesh, Kutupalong–Balukhali Expansion Camp located 20 miles out of the town of Cox's Bazaar is often referred to as the 'mega-camp'. It is the world's largest and most densely populated refugee camp. Some 75 per cent of the Rohingya refugees who fled during the latest crisis arrived in August 2017, though there has been a steady inflow thereafter, with the population of the makeshift camp reaching upwards of 900,000 as of September 2019. It is a harsh environment, and as Bangladesh is the second-most natural disaster-prone country in Asia and the Pacific, the camps are located in an area not suitable for safely accommodating the large population and are made up of makeshift tents and fragile shelters made of bamboo, tarpaulin, and plastic on hilly, steep land. Since the beginning of the crisis, more than 50,000 shelters have been erected. Due to heavy congestion, 75 per cent of families have to share their shelters, and 93 per cent of the population in the camps lives below the United Nations High Commissioner for Refugees (UNHCR) emergency standard of 45 square metres per person. Space can be as low as 8 square metres per person in some areas of the mega-camp (Gaynor 2018; Oxfam 2019).

The poor conditions can also be seen in the overflowing latrines and contaminated waters (Oxfam 2019). Overcrowding, indoor cooking, and suboptimal shelters made of plastic have also increased the risk of fire and respiratory infections (Chan, Chiu, and Chan 2018). Within the camps, there is also a severe lack of essential non-food items, including footwear and feminine hygiene products, increasing the risk of sickness, disease, infection, and injury (Chan, Chiu, and Chan 2018). These unsuitable living conditions are further degraded by bad weather, particularly during the monsoon season, when heavy rains cause significant amounts of damage and injuries, as well as making large areas inaccessible and increasing the risk of disease. During the monsoon season, approximately 2.5 metres of rain falls in a three-month period, 'turning camps built of dusty soil into unhealthy swamps' (Oxfam 2019). Efforts have been made to fortify the land and secure homes with sandbags to prevent landslides and flooding; however, conditions remain the same with each passing monsoon season as flimsy shelters are washed away during storms (Gaynor 2018). Additionally, rain and flooding, poor water drainage, and plastic shelters increase the accumulation of stagnant water, creating breeding sites for disease-carrying flies and mosquitoes (Chan, Chiu, and Chan 2018). Poor weather often makes access to water, food, toilets, aid, and services nearly inaccessible.

At the time of my fieldwork, there was no boundary fence encircling the camps that would distinguish them from other areas of the rural landscape. Yet, as you approach the entrance of the camps, there is a state-manifested perception of a securitized boundary with the wider system of surveillance, which includes a network of internal and external intelligence officers who manage the entry and exit to the camp (Gaynor 2018). The formal security vigilance is less rigorous, however, than one would expect, as the sheer volume of people that have entered the camp grounds has exceeded so much that it is generally easy to circumvent border guards.

Since the first wave of refugees into Bangladesh in 1977, the Rohingyas have largely been settled in two small camps set up by the UNHCR in Nayapara I and II refugee camp located in Teknaf, Bangladesh (further south of Cox's Bazaar) (Bhatia et al. 2018). Eventually, with the recent influx of refugees in August 2017, the Kutupalong–Balukhali expansion mega-camp settlement became the primary area for newly arrived, unregistered Rohingya refugees. This book focuses on the refugees in this particular settlement. This 'temporary city' continues to spread across 5 square miles – a warren of mud paths cut across the vast Kutupalong–Balukhali mega-camp, revealing its unplanned structure, as settlements of fragile, improvised tarpaulin shelters organically grew since Rohingyas fled in the summer of 2017 (Gaynor 2018).

Conclusion

Reflecting on the various avenues I attempted to take in telling this story, like with any ethnographic research, what I have presented within this book has been an exercise in understanding what Michael Jackson (2013) calls 'the politics of storytelling'. And so, in sharing these narratives, while I made every possibility to be collaborative with my participants and ensure that they felt comfortable with the specific stories I was sharing, I have often had to make difficult choices about which stories eventually ended up within the pages of this book. However, as I mapped out the narratives of Rohingya refugee women, what emerged was a clear direction – that of the crucial, emotional, and circumstantial processes that reshaped Rohingya refugee women's sense of self and society. Ultimately, these stories elucidate and help me to stitch together a vibrant portrait of Rohingya women's lives, the ways in which they seek to create a sense of order and meaning within their lives in the refugee camps of Bangladesh, and the aspirations and constraints that shape them.

3

Life Under Siege
On Violence and Displacement

'We Are Rohingyas, We Are the Oppressed'

On a cool, windy evening in March 2018, as the light of dusk spread throughout the vast dusty camps and people began retreating to their shelters, I stood on the edge of a hill with Khatun Khalamma as she tended to a small potted plant of chilli leaves, the chillies beginning to bloom with the arrival of spring. We had been talking for hours – her stories, like that of many refugees like her, vividly encompassed a life of oppression, erasure, and 'running' that were etched into her memory. Tears rolled down her eyes as she fiddled with the chilli plant. She was from Buthidaung township in Rakhine State, Myanmar, and had fled with her son, daughter-in-law, and nine-year-old grandson in the 2017 mass exodus. Her three daughters were raped and killed in Myanmar, and her daughter-in-law died during childbirth once they reached the camps in Bangladesh. The pain of her immense loss and of leaving her homeland was still fresh in her mind. At one point, she began singing a *tarana* (Rohingya song) entitled 'We Are Rohingyas, We Are the Oppressed', which she had heard shared throughout the camp, composed by a fellow Rohingya refugee.

> *We were forced out of our homes*
> *Without rights we sailed away*
>
> *We the women [mothers, sisters] were raped*
> *When we were in Arakan*
>
> *Oh Allah, the Most Gracious, the Most Merciful*
> *Help us in our time of need*
>
> *For how much longer will we remain adrift?*

The *tarana* was haunting, evoking the trauma of displacement and the suppression of their voices when they screamed out to be heard. The life stories of Rohingyas spanned generations, ultimately leading to a migration that was tremendous in its scale and level of desperation. This chapter provides the context to understanding the gendered nature of violence against the Rohingyas and the chaotic nature of their displacement to Bangladesh. By situating the recent migration of Rohingyas from Myanmar to Southeast Asia within the greater context of conflict and systemic violence and oppression in Myanmar's recent history, the chapter is an introduction to the Rohingyas as a borderland people in Myanmar, their life under siege, and provides a glimpse into Rohingya gender relations and roles prior to displacement. Through the voices of those who fled, I trace the journeys of Rohingyas who experienced profound violence and an arduous trek towards the refugee camps in Bangladesh. I recount their horrific experiences in detail to provide a raw account of the events that precipitated their exodus to Bangladesh and also to lay bare the traumatic circumstances from which Rohingya women rebuilt their lives in the refugee camps (discussed in the subsequent chapters).

The Rohingyas in Myanmar

Erasure and Dehumanization

To understand the effects of refugee life on Rohingya women and their families, it is necessary to consider the historical forces and events that brought the refugee community into existence, as well as the deep-rooted political and violent underpinnings that have plagued the Rohingya people for generations (Ibrahim 2016). In 2016, a year prior to the mass exodus of Rohingya refugees to Bangladesh, Azeem Ibrahim published a landmark study on the history of the Rohingya people, detailing the successive generations of intense discrimination, violence, and abuses they have faced at the hands of the Burmese state (Ibrahim 2016). Ibrahim warned that international indifference towards the Rohingyas could have catastrophic consequences as their situation 'stands on the edge of genocide' (Ibrahim 2016: 16). Tragically, his premonitions came true as a year later, in August 2017, over 700,000 Rohingyas were expelled from their native lands in Myanmar and driven into refugee camps in neighbouring Bangladesh.

The Rohingyas are a people who trace their historical and ancestral roots to the Arakan region (present-day Rakhine State) from the seventh century, and their social and cultural associations to the postcolonial boundaries of present-day Myanmar, which was a British colony up to 1984, as well as Bangladesh (then East Pakistan), which became independent from Pakistan in 1971 (Farzana 2011, 2017; Zarni and Cowley 2014). In pre-colonial history, however, the Arakan region was once an independent kingdom separated from 'the Burmese kingdoms in the Irrawaddy delta and central Burma, as well as from Bengal and the Mogul empire to the west' (Farzana 2011: 42). Geographically, the land inhabited by the Arakan kingdom extended as far as Chittagong, which is now part of Bangladesh. Due to the lack of a distinct geographic and physical separation between the Arakan region and Chittagong, Bengali influence in the Arakan region is apparent (Farzana 2011; Ibrahim 2016; Uddin 2020).

However, Burmese Buddhists refute the Rohingyas' historical claims to the region, and the 1948 post-independent Burmese governments did not formally recognize the Rohingyas as an ethno-linguistic group in Myanmar. Their identity was attacked and vilified in a methodical and orchestrated manner by the anti-Muslim government regimes that were controlled by the Tatmadaw (Myanmar military) since 1962, claiming that Rohingya Muslims were more recent 'illegal immigrants' who had arrived in Myanmar from neighbouring Bangladesh. As Farzana (2011: 62) suggests, Myanmar's military government failed to 'differentiate between the Arakanese Muslims who had been in the region for centuries – long before the arrival of the British – from the migrant Muslims who came only in the later part of Burma's [Myanmar's] colonial history'.

In 1978, following an anti-Rohingya campaign by the military junta characterized by bigotry, prejudice, and the denial of citizenship, coupled with the rise of Buddhist extremism, there was an increase in violence, harassment, and arrests. As a result of these processes, the Rohingyas were stripped of their citizenship as the 1982 Burma Citizenship Act failed to recognize them as one of the country's official 135 distinct ethnic groups. There are now less than 500,000 Rohingya Muslims remaining in Myanmar today, and they remain unrecognized and without citizenship, effectively leaving them stateless (Robinson and Rahman 2012; Letchamanan 2013; Al Jazeera 2016; Ibrahim 2016). Since officially being stripped of citizenship in 1982, what followed was mass annihilation and genocide of the Rohingyas at the hands of the Myanmar government, which 'intentionally formulated, pursued, and executed national and state-level plans' aimed at destroying the Rohingya people, thereby leading to a 'deep assault on the identity, culture, social foundation, and history of the Rohingya who are a people with a distinct ethnic culture' (Zarni and Cowley 2014: 682). Part of this dehumanization process began with discriminatory policies enforced by the government to ensure that Rohingyas are officially referred to as 'Bengali' – locally viewed as a racist reference (Robinson and Rahman 2012; Ibrahim 2016).

Rohingya women and men all stressed the blatant racism and discrimination they faced, particularly when it came to the use of the word 'Bengali'. One elderly man, Monir Dada, who lived through much of the initial years of oppression after 1962, told me something that resonated with many of my interlocutors:

> I am old enough to remember when they first started calling us 'Bengali'. We did not understand why they were saying that because most of us did not even know anything about Bangladesh when we were small. But when we learned what it meant, it was difficult for us to accept. We are Rohingya – we have our own identity and culture and language. The Burmese government does not even acknowledge that there is something called Rohingya. Our entire identity is erased from public knowledge in the country. The word 'Rohingya' was completely erased from existence and we never mentioned the word in public. We only talked about it at home. We had to have a secret identity because they erased us.

Similarly, one of my interlocutors Amena, who is in her early forties, remembers the hate slurs she endured from ethnic Rakhine neighbours:

> We used to be called *kala*. I grew up hearing that I must be killed because I am a *kala* and that I must go back to Bangladesh.

The word *kala*, technically meaning 'black', is commonly used as a racial slur in Myanmar, referring to anyone with a darker complexion – especially as ethnic Bangladeshis are darker than ethnic Burmese and Rohingyas bear physical similarities to ethnic Bangladeshis. This 'us versus them' rhetoric represented an attempt at unifying Myanmar under a homogenous culture, language, and religion – namely Burmese and Buddhist – leaving the Rohingyas out of the fold. As the dehumanization of Rohingyas continued through the complete erasure of their identity in public consciousness, so too did it take place in more material ways. Dehumanization based on religion and ethnicity was only one part of the crisis that caused forced displacement. During the military junta rule in 1988, the State Law and Order Restoration Council (SLORC) established military cantonments in Rakhine State, worked to forcefully take land from the Rohingyas without compensation, and also increased threats if they tried to fight back (Robinson and Rahman 2012). Land-grabbing was a collaborative effort by state agencies, multinational businesses, and the army to evict the Rohingyas from the resource-rich Rakhine State. In the period during and following the 1990 election, 'persecution in the form of physical and mental torture such as beatings as well as killings, abduction and rape, economic exclusion, and restrictions on physical movement threatened their livelihood security and physical security' (Farzana 2011).

There was extreme control by the government on Rohingyas' general mobility; as well, they were denied freedom of education and healthcare. Many of the refugees I met in the camps explained that the inability to move freely in Myanmar and the fear of being arrested for attempting to leave their townships to get treatment in hospitals and clinics for medical care resulted in several deaths of family members. Amena recounted the horrific experience of losing her two children during late-stage pregnancies as a result of complications due to not being able to access a clinic. She cried heavily as the memories came back to her:

> My babies died. I was living in hell. Two times this happened. We were not allowed to travel between villages, townships, and outside Rakhine State. If we wanted to go to some other town, we needed to get permits from the NaSaKa [Myanmar border police force] which is part of the Immigration Department. The village leader also needed to give their permission. Both times I needed to go to a hospital because of complications with my pregnancies, but the nearest doctor was in another township. My family did not have enough money to pay for the travel permits as they used to always set the price very high. My situation deteriorated and I lost my babies both times. Tell me, how is that okay? They killed us in our own homes every day like this.

Even seemingly mundane activities like travelling have been greatly stifled because of permits and their exorbitant fees (Mahmood et al. 2016). In addition, their religious freedom was also attacked as mosques were burned down or desecrated, and the *waqf* (endowment) of mosque lands was appropriated (Palmer 2011: 105). The government commenced a two-child policy in 2015 that applied only to Rohingyas, also requiring 36 months to pass between births as a means of dealing with the alleged 'population problem' (Blomquist 2016; Ripoli et al. 2017). In addition, they required expensive permits for marriage or registering their children (Mahmood et al. 2016).

These permits were required only for Rohingyas – fellow Rakhine Buddhists as well as other minority groups were not subject to such rules, including prior permission from the government authorities in order to get married. However, prior permission itself may not have been a problem if authorities did not also demand large amounts in taxes from those who sought permission. One couple, Ahmed and Momtaz Khatun, recalled the time when they were getting married in 1996 and the devastatingly difficult process of simply waiting to get permission. Ahmed said, shaking his head:

Okay, we needed to get permission – that is fine – but they also made that process so difficult for us. The taxes they put on us just to get married, which is a normal part of life, was unbearable and unnecessary. My Buddhist neighbours didn't have any problems. But for us Rohingyas, there was always lots of problems on top of the thousands of other problems we faced. We first needed a *Lathaung* [marriage permission letter that Rohingyas were required to obtain from the military prior to marriage] to get married. Otherwise, we were beaten and fined for getting married. Money was needed when getting married. You needed about 1 lakh *kyat* [equivalent to about 75 USD]. After that, you needed to pay another 1 or 2 lakhs to prepare the documents. And you can't marry before 18-years-old – if you married secretly, the government would come and beat you and then give you fine. When my and Momtaz's families agreed to our wedding it was 1993 – me, my father, and my uncle went to the NaSaKa several times to get the permission and register for the marriage. They asked us to pay 100,000 *kyat* which was even on the lower end of it. Some of my friends were paying more than 300,000 *kyat*. And the first time they told us to come back again with the money. We returned and again they told us to wait. Many times, we would go again and again. I think in total we went six times. Finally in the middle of 1996 they gave us permission, thanks to Allah. The whole process was just unbearable.[1]

Throughout my time in the camps, I continuously heard horrific stories of being effectively 'trapped' in a vicious system of state-sponsored, institutionalized discrimination likened to apartheid. One young man told me in between tears, 'We were living in hell in Rakhine State. Forget about human rights. It was as though we were not even human. We were like animals in a cage confined to Rakhine State only.' Rohingyas all spoke of a life in virtual imprisonment that had profound negative effects on their way of life, including facing extreme poverty, no access to education, as well as constant threats and monitoring by police and local Rakhine vigilante groups. This 'open-air prison' system further faced severe suppression by Buddhist Burmese monks, who were instrumental in blocking humanitarian aid to Rohingyas in Myanmar (Al Jazeera 2016).

The First 'Boiling Point'

In recent years two major waves of extreme violence against the Rohingyas in Myanmar's Rakhine State resulted in the severe humanitarian crisis we see today – namely in 2012 and 2017. In June 2012, tensions in 12 townships in Rakhine State reached a boiling point and were a turning point in the persecution of the Rohingyas. On 28 May, a 27-year-old Rakhine Buddhist woman was allegedly robbed, raped, and then murdered in Ramri township. Three Rohingya men were promptly arrested at the behest of locals. At the same time, Rakhine activists began circulating pamphlets calling for retribution against the Rohingyas. The government sought to depict the situation as one of 'intercommunal violence'. However, reports showed that the attacks targeting the Rohingyas were sponsored and amplified by the military (Ripoli et al. 2017).

25 August 2017 and the 'Clearance Operations'

> It seemed like the world was ending. Everything was gone and destroyed. There was nothing left. I felt like it was time for *Qiyamat* [Day of Judgement].

These were the words spoken by 19-year-old Zannat, who vividly recalls the day that tipped the scale as the most brutal of oppressions against the Rohingyas – of extreme sexual and gender-based violence, as documented by a report to the UNHCR (OHCHR 2017). The Rohingyas faced systematic discrimination, violence, and various forms of government oppression, which had resulted in the degradation of their community. Thus, in the morning hours of 25 August, the Arakan Rohingya Salvation Army (ARSA) launched multiple attacks on a military base and some 30 security outposts across northern Rakhine State. Within hours, the Myanmar military responded by surrounding hundreds of villages across Maungdaw, Buthidaung, and Rathedaung, calling the mission 'clearance operations'. Rakhine communities also aided the military in surrounding these Rohingya villages.

In the days and weeks following 25 August 2017, a disaster quickly unfolded, one that was long in the making. Ayesha, in her late thirties – who now lives in the Rohingya refugee camps in Bangladesh with her elderly father – recalled the horrific scene she bore witness to. With deep, tired eyes, she spoke in between tears, occasionally stopping to stare blankly at the mud walls of her small shelter. She told me:

> When I left my house, the Burmese army and the Mog [the Rakhine people in Myanmar] surrounded our village in Buthidaung township and started shooting uncontrollably. The Mog slaughtered our Rohingya people. My brother was shot dead by them. I witnessed it. We could not find any peace in Burma. People were thrown into fires and burned by launcher attacks, bombs were thrown into our village which is beside a river. We just saw the blood, we could not see the dead bodies. The dead bodies were put into sacks and taken away during the night. That day in August the army and Mog terrorized us more

than they did before. We could not stand it anymore. They told us: this is not your country. You are not from here. You are Bangladeshi. Many people were killed. More than 200 people in my village only. The number of children killed were 100–150. Women were tortured and raped. When I recall what happened in Burma, I want to cry loudly. When my husband was trying to escape, they shot at him. He was still alive, but they slaughtered him. He was carrying two of our children. They shot my husband. They took my children and threw them away. They died.

Noor Alom, a man in his late thirties, similarly remembers watching his 'beautiful, thatched home' being burned to the ground, as well as the homes of all his neighbours. He recalled:

I woke up at 3 a.m. and my neighbour's house was on fire. I was rushing to find my pregnant wife, but then the Mog came into the house and dragged my wife and raped her in front of my eyes. She was pregnant with our first child. Then they beat me continuously with the back of their guns one by one and kicked me out of the house before burning it. They forced me to watch as they burnt the house with my pregnant wife inside who had just been raped. [*Silence for a while as Noor Alom is crying.*] I couldn't save her. I couldn't save our home. They burnt everything. Our village was one of the first ones that the army attacked in Rakhine State. Everything was completely burnt down. They burnt down the small clinic also. The government lied and said we the Rohingya did it to our own homes – now tell me why would we do that? The army and the Mog ruined everything. They ruined our lives and forced us out of our homes.

There were countless narratives like this – my interlocutors openly shared their difficult memories, bearing witness to mass killings and tactics of violence that were part of a 'deliberate, well-planned strategy to intimidate, terrorize and punish the Rohingya' (OHCHR 2017: 19; D'Costa 2018). Many Rohingyas explained that in numerous villages people were killed or injured by targeted or indiscriminate gunshot, often as they fled from burning houses. Others were killed in arson attacks, or in Noor Alom's wife's case, burned to death in their own homes, as elderly persons, those with disabilities, and small children had greater difficulty escaping.

In the village of Tula Toli in particular, the clearance operation was especially brutal as mass killings were perpetrated, so much so that the incident is referred to as the 'Tula Toli massacre'. My interlocutors told me that on the morning of 30 August 2017, the Myanmar army and local Rakhine villagers blocked off all the exit points. One woman, who wished not to be named, was the only surviving member of her family, as all her family members were murdered that fateful day in Myanmar. She covered her face with her shawl as she recounted the events of that day:

> Hundreds were killed that day. So many of them were children. I lost my parents and my five siblings in Tula Toli. But I was outside my house when the army came so I ran behind a tree and hid. The Mog was using megaphones and shouting loudly: 'You do not belong here – go back to Bangladesh. If you do not leave, we will torch your houses and kill you.' I was hiding behind the tree when the Mog came and killed my father and younger brother with gunshots. I saw the Mog beat them up with guns and sticks. Then one of them kicked my father on his head and I saw the blood coming out. [*She stops for a few minutes.*] I was hiding and so scared. I couldn't do anything. The Mog kept firing and firing at my family. They gathered my mother, my two younger sisters, lots of other women in the village, and took them to a house. I saw the army take the women inside the building five at a time and they remained inside maybe an hour or so. I don't know what they did with them, but I know it was *bolazuri zulm* [rape] ... [*she trails off*]. After a while, the army came out and set the house on fire. There were maybe 300 women and girls – they were all inside and they all were murdered. That's when I started to run. I remember at night from the hillside I saw our villages burning – one house after another, and anybody who would return to the village was attacked by the Mog.

Very few survived the massacre of Tula Toli. The number of deaths was so high that bodies were transported using military vehicles, burned, and then discarded in mass graves. The clearance operations were especially harrowing because of the methodical and systematic use of rape and sexual violence.

The Gendered Nature of Violence: War on Women's Bodies

As part of the 'clearance operations', there was a clear targeted and intentional attack against women and girls, and many of my interlocutors felt that violence against women was a specific tactic used by the military. The OHCHR (2017: 19) states that these clearance operations were 'only possible in a climate of long-standing tolerance and impunity, where military personnel had no reasonable fear of punishment or disciplinary action', and thus rape and sexual violence against women was used in a methodical and systematic manner. Rape, as in other conflicts around the world, was used as a means of eliminating minority groups (Hyndman and de Alwis 2004). Similarly, for the Rohingya, each wave of violence entailed systematic and widespread sexual and gender-based violence against Rohingya women and girls. An elder in the community, Nur Imam, spoke at length, repeating his sentences, angry at the injustices his people faced:

> It was a clear tactic the Myanmar army used against the Rohingya. First they targeted our women with *zulm*. They know that we the men will fight back and start leaving our homes to help the women. When they started creating fear in our minds, we saw the Mog taking our women and girls and raping them, so we left our homes and then the Mog thought that we wouldn't need our houses anymore. We needed to save the women and our family's reputation and our honour. Then they took over our homes and burned them down, and in the end we are left with nothing. So, we left our homes. We left our land. I will tell whoever will listen … again and again. They raped the young women. They slaughtered and killed the young men. They launched rockets at our house. They gathered people to burn them from one side and kill them from the other. They killed and burned us. If anyone survived, they were taken into military custody. They took the men that stood against them, but why did they harm the women and children? What were their crimes?

Another man, Arif, described the chilling scene he was forced to witness after the Myanmar army stormed his village in Buthidaung township.

> When the soldiers came my sister was in the front room. They grabbed her right away before I could save her as I was in the other room. Two soldiers pinned me against the wall while three others were doing *zulm* on her. They gang-raped her in front of me. Then they threw hot water on my body and I was burning all over. But my sister was suffering more than me. I could see her struggling to break free but one after the other they continued to oppress her. They hit her so many times with their guns and then she was gone. The soldiers left me there to burn thinking I was going to die.

Similarly, Shofika, a 19-year-old woman who now lives in the Rohingya camps with her older brother, Kobir – the only other surviving member of her family – sat quietly with me one morning. Kobir also sat nearby; his head was down as she recalled the moment after she started running from her village:

> After I saw the Mog killed my family, all I did was run. I was just running and continued to run until I saw maybe 50 to 60 women inside a school building and the army were bringing more inside. I feared being raped, so I started running in another direction. That way they could not find me to rape me. But I know the women in the school were raped, tortured, and their breasts were cut off. After the military left, most were dead.

As Shofika's testimony highlights, the army had a clear 'mission' to gather women in large groups to specific areas (such as a hut, school, and so on) for mass rapes. Survivors of these mass rapes described being subjected to other sexual assaults, such as breast mutilation. Some of my interlocutors noted that the violence was not derived – at least solely – from individual sexual desire but rather a group effort to dehumanize and violate their sense of self.

Twenty-two-year-old Hasna was one such victim of a group rape. We sat alone in her shelter as she removed the baby pink shawl from her body and picked up her *bazu* (dress) to show me the long, deep gash where a bullet had struck her on her thigh. Other marks on her body exposed her scars of rape and sexual violation – one of her breasts had been cut severely. We cried together and sat in silence for 20 minutes. She later told me that while she felt immense shame, she wanted me to see it.

> When I think about it, my hands and legs start shivering. I feel dizzy. I cannot sleep. The pain here and here [*gesturing to her breast and thigh*] is unbearable. I cry and cry for many hours until I have nothing left to cry about. And then I get angry because I remember everything that happened. I try to forget but every single thing is fresh in my mind as though it happened just now. When the Tatmadaw took me there were eight or nine other women with me. We were taken to a home where they first hit us with sticks and guns. I was beaten again and again on my head and fell to ground. I saw another woman who was holding her baby and … [*she pauses for some time, crying*] they grabbed the baby … *ya Allah ya Allah* … what can I tell you, they completely sliced the baby in half. Then they began raping all of us – there was 14 or 15 men altogether gathered around us, taking off our clothes. We struggled so much and scratched them. But if we tried to fight back they kept beating us. I was fighting a lot. That's when one of them cut me so deeply on my breast. I was bleeding badly but that didn't stop them. They kicked me so hard and that is when my leg broke. I could not stand up. I was lying down on the floor when one by one the men came on top of me. All the women in the room were raped by different men – some of them came from the other women and started to rape me. I only remember the last thing was being shot by a bullet on my thigh because I was trying to kick one of them. Many of the women were dead. They left me there also thinking I was dead. I became unconscious and I don't know what happened after that.

Hasna expressed that she was grateful to be alive and was reunited with her father once they reached the camps. But her story, like that of many other Rohingya women, is testament to the fact that sexual assault and rape at the hands of the Myanmar army were systematically used as weapons against the

Rohingya community. This grave suffering was a profound trauma that was felt in the unuttered words and prolonged silences of my interlocutors. Some expressed shame; others expressed anger; still others had learned to hide their emotions with laughter. There were several instances where my interlocutors chose not to dwell on the past, despite the wounds still fresh – 'I don't want to think about those things. Let's talk about our life now. What is gone is gone', one of my interlocutors, Karima, sighed. It is these painful moments of remembrance, the prolonged silences, and the interrupted testimonies that serve as a reminder that they are not merely victims but survivors.

A Humanitarian Crisis Unfolds

The Chaos of Flight

After the violence, burnings, and subjugation, a million desperate journeys began. Rohingyas left their villages and homes behind, setting off on a dangerous and precarious journey, not knowing exactly where their destination would be, but nonetheless, out of necessity, following one another in search of refuge.

> After the Mog came to our village they took my husband, brother, and 10-year-old son. My brother managed to escape somehow and came to find me and my mother and told us the Mog was coming to rape the women. It was torture. There was so much pain everywhere and some of my neighbours, my two aunts and their children, and a few others from the village – we all started running together. We didn't know where we were going – we just saw others from other villages also running so we followed them. When nighttime came it was pitch dark and we heard there were Mog waiting to catch Rohingyas, so we hid for many hours behind some trees. It was 15 days that we were hiding in the trees, trying to make our way to Bangladesh. We tried to get to the other side of the river, but then the boat stopped working. Water started coming inside the boat. One of my neighbours from my village, her mother, son, and daughter all were in the boat and they all drowned. We tried again the next night – we had to move only at night to avoid being shot by the Mog and Burmese military. We had no water to drink, no food, nothing. My feet became very swollen but there was no chance to stop. I had to help carry my mother during many parts since she was unable to keep up. *Afa*, what can I say … it was horrible and scary. We were so exhausted and hungry. In the dark when we were crossing, we could hear noises and every time we would think the Mog is coming after us again. After 15 days we arrived on Shahpuri Island, which is at the mouth of the river. We stayed there for a few days. That was the first point for us when we arrived

to Bangladesh. We stayed in a *madrassa* [Islamic religious school] for many days. At that time, we were all confused about where to go next. I was with my family and some of the families from my village. Many others were there too from other villages and we were all waiting to see what is the next step. Because we reached Shahpuri Island at night, it was very dark and quiet and we were not sure if we were even in the right direction. But at the *madrassa* they gave us food and some shelter for a few days, and then we started moving again. Another friend from my village was with us – she lost her two babies who drowned when our boat first capsized in the river. Another *khalamma* [elderly grandma] could not continue and collapsed and died from the running. There was so much death all around us. I cannot bear it.

This was the experience of 35-year-old Zomila, who recounted the chaos of fleeing from Myanmar, traversing the countryside by foot and arriving at the camps. Zomila became a trusted interlocutor of mine – her perilous journey by boat and foot was similar to the stories of others, where chaos and death erupted as families scrambled to flee from their villages. As her moving account illustrates, displacement was not linear; rather, it was messy and dangerous as refugees moved from one place to another, not knowing exactly where their destination would be. There was uncertainty and risk – especially of being caught by smugglers or traffickers, or worse yet, captured by Burmese soldiers. This was the case of 17-year-old Zaida, who revealed that the Mog raped her mother, sister, niece, and sister-in-law, after which they burned her house down with all of them inside. She fled her village on her way to Bangladesh and walked through the jungle for 15 days before being captured by soldiers and kept in a cell for five days, where she was beaten and raped. She told me:

I was running by myself after I escaped from the cell. It was completely dark and I did not know where I was or where I was going. I only know I was in unbearable pain because the soldiers beat me with a rod, and tied my hands and feet together on a pole for many days. I cannot know how many days exactly – maybe 15. It was a long time. In the beginning I was with some others from my village after my family was killed, but when the military caught me and I was separated from them. When I fought back, they shot my leg.

She showed me the deep scar all across her legs making it difficult for her to walk, and she now uses home-made crutches. She does not remember exactly what happened next, but says that after three days, she found herself next to the Naf River with stab wounds on her face. 'I had to crawl to hide behind a tree for a day. I didn't know who to trust. I was very scared.' The next day another group of fleeing refugees found her and helped carry her across the river to Bangladesh. Another interlocutor, Hafeza, who was in her late teens, told me in a matter-of-fact quick manner:

> We had to leave our home barefoot and everything we had. We left everything behind. When the military attacked our village, we managed to escape. We took a boat across the river in the night and hid ourselves, and like that we managed to flee. I lost by baby in my stomach. My other five month-old baby drowned.

That was all Hafeza wanted to share about her journey. Jackson (2013) suggests that stories by displaced populations about the experiences of flight are sometimes fragmented and devoid of detail. The social context remains untouched, but events that took place over weeks and months become condensed into a few words. As Hannah Arendt (1968) writes, the unsettling events associated with flight are 'unbearable sequences of sheer happening'. But my interlocutors continued to share their stories – in many ways to make sense of what happened and also because 'the world needs to know what happened to us', Zomila told me.

Conclusion

In collecting their narratives, I found that most of my interlocutors spoke vividly and intensely of the suffering they endured – the horrific experiences of violence, gang rape, entire villages being burned down in the process, the extensive nature of violence that the security forces unleashed, and the eventual long and arduous journey of fleeing were fresh. Khatun Khalamma once told me it was because 'it removes a load from my shoulder. My story is now yours and you will now bear witness to it.' As Nancy Scheper-Hughes (2008) suggests, narrativity is often used to reflect upon and recover from one's hardships, sometimes in a way to move forward as well as to deal with the past.

Note

1. 'Lakh' is a unit followed in the South Asian numbering system, where 1 lakh = 100,000.

4

At Journey's End

On Home and Belonging

Arrival to the Camps

There's more! There's more! They're coming! They're coming!

These words echoed throughout the camp one morning in early September 2017. It was just after dawn – the sand had muddied from the torrential monsoon rains the night before, the yellow-orange hue of the sun shining over the soggy terrain. In the distant horizon beyond the sandy expanse and just over the rice paddies, crowds of people emerged out of nowhere – first in tens, then in thousands, until their presence carpeted the entire landscape. Their sunken faces revealed the exhaustion of a prolonged journey, escaping unspeakable calamity only to be faced with an uncertain future. The refugees were hungry and drained, pacing through the scorching heat – some carrying the weight of their children, while others their elderly family members. Some were able to gather a few belongings and bare necessities from their homes in Myanmar at the last minute, which they wrapped inside larger knotted shawls that they carried on their shoulders, the knots clinging for dear life to stay secure. Many others brought nothing with them except the clothes on their backs. Many Rohingya women later recounted to me that they did not know their exact destination, but they ran nonetheless, out of necessity, following one another across dense forest lands until they had reached the camps in search of refuge.

As time passed and days trickled into weeks and then months, the camps became the only place of residence for nearly a million Rohingya refugees. Within this context, Rohingya women have had to negotiate and re-forge community ties as well as renew their understandings of 'self' (Bhabha 1994; Abusharaf 2005, 2009; Fiddian-Qasmiyeh 2014). Though estranged from their native homeland of Myanmar, a sense of 'home' has begun to emerge in the camps from the shared experiences of displacement, the social and cultural interactions that constitute the camps, and the routine activities that provide meaning in their everyday life. This chapter explores the narratives of Rohingya women after being uprooted from Myanmar and forced into refugee camps in Bangladesh. While having lost their homes in Myanmar, Rohingya women have been able to re-establish 'community' and traditions in the refugee camps, thereby creating a sense of home and belonging despite their predicaments. By exploring the lived experiences of Rohingya refugee women, this chapter reveals that even in the direst of circumstances, refugees maintain a productive capacity to transform their setting, thereby producing a new sense of 'home'.

Home, Place, and Belonging

Few events cause as much upheaval in an individual's life as forced migration, as it entails intense rupture and dislocation. A refugee camp is a profoundly new environment for refugee women, who must navigate the new spatial and social dynamics of a cramped, overpopulated environment. As Linda McDowell (1999: 5) writes, 'places are defined, maintained and altered through the impact of unequal power relations'. Refugee women are forced to rebuild their lives in a space where their personal autonomy is greatly limited. In such settings, it is particularly important to pay attention to the tremendous human capacity to not only survive but, as Scheper-Hughes (2008) contends, also 'thrive' despite experiences of violence, deprivation, and profound trauma. As Lawrence Grossberg (2000: 154) notes, belonging involves the active sentiment 'of identification, of involvement and investment, of the line connecting and binding different events together'. Refugee women infuse new meanings into their lives in the camps, despite the limitations of their immediate setting, by continuing practices that appropriate meanings from their past. It is through the appropriation and reshaping of deeply held personal, communal, and social meanings that Rohingya women are able to recreate a sense of order and belonging in their lives in displacement, thereby creatively recasting their environment as a familiar setting with intimate meanings.

To understand and analyse the way 'home' and 'belonging' are experienced by Rohingya refugees, this chapter employs the notion of 'placemaking' that Julie Peteet (2005) uses to explore the relationship between space and society. In her research on Palestinian refugees in Lebanon, Peteet (2005: 93) contends that refugees engage in the 'social production of place', whereby new meanings and understandings are created 'by the regular, patterned activities and social relationships that unfold in it and the cultural rules governing them'. Place is thus governed and juxtaposed by the cultural and social space that it encompasses, a 'not only context-driven but also context-generative' experience, as articulated by Appadurai (1996: 186). This notion is particularly useful to understanding the ways in which Rohingya refugees took up placemaking projects in Bangladesh after displacement.

The issues relating to space, place, and home are a primary locus of discussion for refugees dislocated from their countries of origin and forced into camps. As David Turton (2005: 258) argues, making a place for oneself involves the production of individual localized meanings, and thus the emergence of a sense of community within refugee camps follows patterns that reflect both existing familiar and wider social structures and the disruption to these structures resulting from displacement. Peteet (2016) further contends that the profound experiences of displacement play a defining role in the spatial and temporal meanings that animate life and social relations in the camp. While refugees face 'social paralysis' due to the general lack of opportunities and livelihoods, as well as extensive dependence on outside parties, they nonetheless are capable of adapting to their environment (Peteet 2016). This may entail the transformation of their environment and thus the circumstances that they inhabit. Alice Corbet (2016) demonstrates that refugees, in adapting to their new settings, may bring into existence 'new social forms and opportunities' through their everyday practices. New identities unfold and emerge in the camp setting, which Gupta and Ferguson (1997: 13) assert are a 'mobile, often unstable relation of difference', particularly evident amongst refugees. For refugees, place is a lived experience – moving as they move from village to camp, country to country – carrying stories, identities, a sense of 'home'. Thus, despite the setbacks and limitations brought about by circumstances in the camp, refugees possess the capacity to reorient their environment by adapting new meanings and, ultimately, a renewed sense of self. And indeed, identities – whether gendered or otherwise – are 'positional, strategic, and relational' (Peteet 2016). As in Palestinian refugee camps in Lebanon, place and identity have been mutually constitutive, as Peteet (2005: 100) succinctly notes:

> Identities and affiliations, belonging to a particular group whether family or village, nuanced the process by which camps became places of attachment and identification. In turn, those identities were profoundly transformed by life in these bounded spaces.

Using Peteet's placemaking project in the refugee context, in this chapter I extend her arguments by adding the gender lens, acknowledging that placemaking – and, by extension, the experience of 'home' and 'belonging' in displacement – is heavily gendered. Gendered norms of space and mobility are thus important and necessary to placemaking and play a significant role in the way gendered identities are negotiated. My analysis looks at how displacement and forced migration both shape and are shaped by these social processes, thereby transforming gender relations that allow for transformative gendered experiences amongst Rohingya refugee women. The remainder of this chapter illustrates the re-establishment of life after migration, where bonding and kinship and social organization were of utmost importance, and thus engages with Rohingya women's profound, productive actions as they craft a sense of 'home' and 'place', and, in the process, adapt their gendered identities and subjectivities. There was a desire for social continuity in the formation of community and the way social relations and practices shaped the physical and social environment to 'impose symbolic meaning on place' (Peteet 2005: 107).

Settling in the Camp

In the days following that harrowing scene of arrival, the urgency of flight from Myanmar translated into a frenzy of disorder in the camps – its size swelling exponentially as refugees continued to arrive – and the chaos was evident in the way the refugee camps were set up. The early days of their arrival were the most difficult; one by one, families were grouped and regrouped by NGOs and aid organizations that operated around the clock as thousands more Rohingyas arrived in the quiet of the night, confused and disoriented. The way the refugees were 'settled into the camps' (the words used by my interlocutor Zannat), with little time to think about how daily life would unfold in the coming days and months, was a reminder of the way self and community were negotiated and renegotiated. 'Home' was crafted in the way social and cultural nuances were engendered onto space and created in meaningful daily relations stemming from the relationships enacted through the process of displacement and encampment (Peteet 2005; Omata 2016).

It was shortly after the first large wave of arrivals in late August 2017 when I first met Zomila (introduced in Chapter 3). I witnessed her arrival with her elderly mother and brother, their eyes glazed over from the horrific acts they had witnessed. Her husband and son were killed in Myanmar during the brutal onslaught, and many of her neighbours were also killed when the Burmese army descended upon their village without forewarning. The group she arrived with had travelled for two weeks through thickets and rivers – many in the group now unable to stand upright out of sheer exhaustion.

They were received by the UNHCR and other NGOs, local communities, and the Bangladesh government.

When the refugees first arrived in the camps, the land was cloaked in jungle. As the 2017 wave of refugees was exponentially greater than any prior period of refugee arrival, the initial days after arrival, the atmosphere was chaotic. Convoys of overfilled UNHCR trucks were rolling in every few hours with support from the Bangladeshi army, both working around the clock to build dirt roads to allow greater aid access. Construction agencies had been called in to stabilize the landslide-prone hills, where incoming refugees would eventually settle. The UNHCR, with the cooperation of local communities in surrounding villages as well as with the help of newly arrived Rohingyas themselves, cleared away large swaths of trees – including portions of protected nature preserve – to be able to provide building materials and wood as fuel for cooking. They broke away large mounds of sand to set up the makeshift tarpaulin shelters.

Many of my interlocutors shared (as highlighted in Chapter 2) that initially families and neighbours from the same village fled together and tried to remain together during the arduous journey across the Myanmar countryside. However, many families were separated from their group when hiding in the pitch-black of the night. Others broke off as they progressed more slowly to accommodate the elderly amongst them. Other communities began to splinter when crossing the Naf River into Bangladesh on rickety, overpacked boats. Arrival into the camps was varied, and the 'settling in' process depended on the time of arrival as well as the location of available shelters. The UNHCR and local organizations worked to settle refugees into various 'zones' as they arrived, with an appointed (unelected) Rohingya member referred to as a *majhee*, the head of each zone and a camp leader, who is responsible for acting as a liaison with various officials. These *majhee*s – all men, mostly in their thirties or forties – were installed by the Bangladeshi army as a stopgap measure, although their role as 'block leaders' continued thereafter. They served as intermediaries with aid organizations and dealt with local issues or community governance matters within their specific zone.

On the evening that Zomila and her family had arrived at the camps, she was gathered with 100 other refugees in the receiving area to await news of where they would be placed next. A UNHCR worker looked after the group of newly arrived refugees and told them that the *majhee* would take them to their designated area and set them up there. Another woman in her early twenties, Aleya, who was Zomila's neighbour in their village in Myanmar, had been part of the same group that journeyed to the camps and later told me how the 'distribution' of refugees took place:

> When we came to the camp, it was chaos. We were standing for hours in line waiting to be put into locations and then we were given bamboo sticks and tarp to set up our own shelters. There were so many of us. I was still with my family but some of my neighbours who we came with were separated when we were walking for days in the rice paddies. Many of them died. Altogether from my village there were four families – though most had missing family members – and we were put into this area in this group of huts with some of the families that we met along the way. Everything was just crazy then and we didn't know what was going to happen to us. We followed the *majhee* who brought the group of us to this area in the camp and now we are settled here. It was better for us to be with some families that we know – at least one or two – it is better than knowing nobody. I heard later on that more families from my village came to the camps a few weeks after us but they are settled elsewhere. So now there are many people from different villages here. But we are all from neighbouring villages as many of us came from the same area in Maungdaw township.

After being taken by the *majhee* to their designated zone, the refugees' first task, as Aleya notes, was to begin the difficult work of constructing their shelters. The very act of establishing camps and constructing the dwelling – the bamboo and tarp shelter – for individual families was, as Peteet (2005: 111) asserts, the 'most basic features of placemaking', as it served as the endpoint of an arduous journey and the beginning of a new episode of life. The shelter served as the foundation from which new possibilities could emerge. In the case of Palestinian refugees, Peteet's (2005) research revealed that camps were organized according to the village of origin as well as neighbourhoods within a specific village – a settlement pattern that attempted to socially recreate 'lost villages'. The process allowed for 'placemaking' that integrally depended on existing villages and clan units. In the case of Rohingya refugees however, settling in was more haphazard. As some families managed to travel together, they were already clustered, thus allowing those families from the same village to end up in the same zone. However, of the families under a single *majhee*, only a handful would end up in the same village – the others being strangers to one another, though possibly coming from the same township (and all sharing the harrowing experience of forced displacement). With the sudden arrival of such a significant volume of refugees in such a short period of time, the Bangladeshi government and official organizations prioritized the act of providing any feasible place of shelter – a formidable task in itself – to those refugees rather than keeping communities intact. Majed, the *majhee* in charge of Zomila and Aleya's zone, explained:

> When the crisis began in the August 2017, much of the migration happened in waves. So, you will find that let's say an attack took place in a village in Myanmar at the end of August, at the time maybe 4–5 families left their village, which is about on average 5 members per family. So, you can say from one village about 25 members from the same village came during that wave and once they reached the camp they were waiting in lines or in groups with 4–5 families from another village, or others they met along the way. Like that different families came in waves, and because the migration was very chaotic many people came at one time, and we tried our best to divide them as best as we can. These are not registered refugees so there is no concept of registering and then nicely putting everyone in their preferred location with all their neighbours from their home village or even their relatives. So, you will see that many families have relatives in another makeshift camp 10 or 30 minutes away. When the crisis happened that time with the thousands and thousands of refugees coming every day, our main – and only – goal, was to give them shelter right away.

With the haphazard nature of arrival, government officials and NGOs worked alongside *majhee*s with the principal objective of providing shelter. While members from the same village would have ideally preferred to be housed in the same area, the nature of the settlement process did not lend to this level of organization. Within any given area, a *majhee* would be responsible for 90–120 refugees (or 20–25 families), and among them, 4 or 5 families may have come from the same village in Myanmar. In some cases, families may have met during a flight across the countryside. While families attempted to create a semblance of 'home' in exile by remaining connected to and settling alongside families from the same village, the chaos of flight, and death and dispersal of relatives, caused each section of the camp to be dotted with families from various villages.

Over time, I witnessed that as Rohingyas began to settle, they began looking for missing family members, relatives, and fellow villagers. These efforts provided the initial steps towards re-establishing social ties and creating a semblance of community in the camps. Through these patchwork efforts of community building, fragmented lives were woven together through a renegotiation of gender identities and social norms in an attempt to find belonging and ultimately 'home'. The rest of this chapter demonstrates how a 'relational home' and community were re-established, arising from the lived experiences of refugees that emerge from the interactions and connections they forge with others in their new setting. While there is dislocation, there is also a 'practical' creation of home and belonging through 'new fictive kin relations based on common experiences during displacement rather than only on blood' (Grabska 2010: 254). These 'home-making' experiences were highly gendered and imbued with personal meanings.

Shifting Subjectivities

Re-creating Home, Re-creating Community

It was late December 2017, and the weather was cool and windy in the camps as the evening settled over the dusty valley of orange tarpaulin dwellings. In the days after being 'allocated' to their respective zones of the camp and setting up their shelters, refugees began looking for their lost family members. Locating family members occurred by word of mouth – most refugees did not bring cellphones with them when they fled Myanmar; and thus they were considered a luxury as very few in the camps – and even fewer women – possessed one. Furthermore, as the camps were still in the process of being developed, formidable challenges existed in navigating the labyrinth of unmarked, undifferentiated shelters without getting lost.

Shofika (introduced in Chapter 2) and I stood in front of her shelter as the bustle of the market below took place. After weeks of inquiring with everyone she knew, Shofika received news that her older brother Kobir was at the other end of the Kutupalong–Balukhali mega-camp. At the time, Shofika was living with her aunt and her family after she managed to escape from the village when all her other family members were killed. With the news that Kobir was alive, Shofika suddenly regained a glimmer of hope that had all but disappeared since escaping Myanmar:

> I need to find him. I have nobody left. When we were all together under one roof in one country, what a beautiful time it was. I didn't see him for so many months now. But if I can find him then I will feel like I have my family with me. I will know I am not alone. In our culture, we like to be with our family and all our relatives. I am now at least with my aunt but my mother and father and siblings – everyone is gone. There is nothing left – only memories of them. You are at peace when you have everyone in your family with you. I am happy to be with my aunt – at least I know I am not alone. She and my little cousins are all I have now. If I can find my brother that will make me happy.

A few weeks after, Shofika and her brother were finally reunited, and they now shared the one room in her aunt's shelter. Another woman, Maleka, who was in search of her son after he was separated when they fled by boats from their village in Buthidaung township, shared her worries, which were echoed by many others:

> We need to be with our family members. Our culture is like that. Home is where everyone remains together – all our brothers, sisters, aunts, cousins, grandparents. It is nice to have everybody together. My daughter was killed in the massacre in our village, then my 15-year-old son was separated when we were fleeing. He was put into another boat from us and now I'm still looking for him. My main priority is to find him so we can be together again.

Rohingya culture is based strongly on communal and kinship ties, and thus one of the main tasks of many families after fleeing to the camps was attempting to reunite with lost family members and re-establish their social networks, which for Shofika and Maleka was an important and necessary process of re-creating 'home'. While 'home' denoted a sense of familial belonging, oftentimes it did not refer only to one's immediate family; rather, it also alluded to the meaning of 'community' consisting of a wider set of social ties and connections. Those unable to find immediate family members and kin members, or whose family members died or disappeared, had to rely on social relations with distant relatives or with members of their village in Myanmar. These social ties radiated across the camps since individuals arrived at different times and were settled into a variety of zones. These ties with individuals that refugees knew in Myanmar were overlaid by new social relations forged with those within one's immediate community in the camps. While previously held social ties could be useful for locating family and maintaining a sense of connection with the past, new social ties within one's immediate physical locality allowed for women to carry out their daily tasks in the camps – whether looking after children, preparing meals, or otherwise. Close physical proximity thus helped bridge social proximity by creating new communities that struggled with common day-to-day issues, as well as sharing the collective pain of being displaced from Myanmar.

In this way, 'home' had been recast in the form of what Naohiko Omata (2016: 28) refers to as a 'relational home' that 'emerges from the lived experiences of refugees through interactions and connections which they forge with other people in a new place'. The notion of home was thus a vital part of the way Rohingya women understood their connection to others and the construction of a community of new fictive kin relations based on common experiences of displacement and exile, which were a pivotal step in establishing oneself in the settlement process. Although one of the outcomes of forced displacement is the 'dismantling of communities' (Cernea 2000), refugees sharing no previous personal relations retain the capacity to forge new social bonds with one another that lead to the formation of new communities (Hammond 2004; Omata 2016). Despite their divergent pasts, refugees in a single locale formed social ties based on common cultural practices as well as shared experiences of displacement. For many refugee women like Shofika and Maleka, community assumes a new meaning as it entails a combination of pre-existing social ties radiating across the camp, alongside new ties with immediate community members who can be relied upon to support them with their everyday lives. The combination creates a sense of social belonging.

Home-Making and Feeling at Home

As the weeks and months wore on, one's immediate community became the foundational social structure for Rohingyas living in the camps. As it was not possible to replicate traditional village settings, where extended families from the same village were housed in the same zone within the camps, this change in settlement patterns affected Rohingya women's gendered subjectivities. Settling in the camps involved gendered negotiations and acquiring new meanings about others as well as oneself within the larger network of society and community. For women, creating a sense of community was critical as they were isolated from the support system of relatives and village neighbours who would have been able to assist them during a problem back in their villages in Myanmar. As families were separated and many extended family members were killed, lost, or living in a farther part of the camp, physical and social isolation from supportive family networks meant re-establishing new ties in a way that would be beneficial for more difficult tasks.

For Rohingya women, personal, family, and community life assumed intimate meanings through mundane everyday practices that include performing group prayers, sharing food with neighbours, forging friendships, attending the mosque, collecting wood, and frequenting the market. Domesticity saturates the lives of Rohingya women, and in many ways, they attempted to recreate that daily rhythm of life in the camps. In their everyday actions, they reconstructed their social worlds replete with intimate meanings. Maleka was cutting some vegetables at the door of her shelter one afternoon, looking out into the camp below. She reminisced about life in Myanmar while vividly reflecting on the nuances of everyday life in exile:

We were happy back in Burma and our village was very beautiful and green. My house in Burma had lots of furniture and other nice things – many special items and beautiful clothing for my children. I had a lot of gold and jewellery. I could only bring a few of those things with me which I had to sew into my *bazu* [dress] all of which I had to sell once we reached here because we had no money... [*she trails off and starts to dig her knife into the mud, digging deeply; a few seconds later she returns to cutting the vegetables after rinsing her knife with a cup of water I hand to her*]. We had lots of friends in Burma and a good life [*she says, while looking out into the camps below*]. But we did not have peace – we were worried for our lives every day and so we ran before the Mog came to our village. Here in the camps it is more or less a better existence than I expected. Things are very difficult and there are so many women, men, children – everyone together in one place so close to each other. But I take care of my children and play with them and we try to be happy. What's the use of holding on to pain? If it comes to mind or I feel bad, I try to forget. I try to keep myself busy and occupied with housework and taking care of my children to take my mind off the pain I feel. Especially when I talk to the women in the shelters around me – my neighbours – we sit together in the afternoon and sew together; sometimes we laugh, help each other to cook. This is how we can go on.

Maleka's narrative provides a glimpse of the routines of everyday life in the camps, where, after facing the trauma of violence and displacement, a steady rhythm of normalcy had begun to settle. Women sit for hours in front of their shelters exchanging stories and banter, decorating themselves and their homes with the adornment available to them – *thanaka* (a yellow-paste makeup native to Myanmar) and other valuable mementos that they brought with them from life before exile. Another interlocutor, Zolekha, remarked:

It is not Burma but we are making a life here. We don't know what the future will be like so we try our best to survive. What else can we do? We don't have our cows and poultry here like we had in our villages – or my vegetable garden – so things are more difficult here. But we are still living our life based on the values and traditions we had back home. Everyday we are cooking and cleaning and being with our children – in many ways it is so different than life in Burma but sometimes I also feel that it's not very different. We don't know how long we will be here, but for now we are still making a life here. [*She suddenly lights up.*] Did you see, *afa*, my photo frame? [*She rushes in to get the frame for her shelter and shows me the beautifully painted frame with pride.*] Look here, isn't it nice? I finally took it out a few days ago – my mother painted it many years ago. I like to decorate my shelter with these small things I brought with me – with those same decorations and traditions.

The spatiality of the camp has dramatically transformed the way interactions take place. Privacy became an issue as everyone now lives in close proximity to one another. In Myanmar, the Rohingyas had homes with plots of land as well as animals they took care of and also depended on for their livelihood. The camps in Bangladesh are thus a radical rupture from the past, as women now face a significant reduction in privacy as well as an inability to sustain themselves with their own resources. Traditionally, women have had limited access to public areas, but in the refugee camps the definition of public and private areas in daily activities is not totally clear. While there are specifically defined public areas such as the bazaar and roadways, the cramped and overcrowded arrangement of shelters has blurred the lines between public and private space (Peteet 2005).

Despite these changes, Rohingya women have been able to establish a sense of 'home' by creating normalcy through the routines of everyday life. Home becomes a setting where daily activities provide a sense of self-worth and meaning, where certain traditions from the past continue while mixing with new practices in the present. The very ability to maintain such routines helps transform a foreign camp into a familiar environment replete with intimate meanings. For Rohingya women, there is food to be made, cleaning to be completed, chores to be finished. These simple, quotidian household tasks are a means of coping and 'carrying on' with life (Gren 2015). Routines, order, and predictability, as Nina Gren (2015) suggests, help individuals deal with crises and difficult circumstances. This mundanity captures the micro-level process that provides Rohingya women a meaningful sense of attachment to their new setting. Similarly, Janice Goodman (2004) found that refugees in Sudan distracted themselves and suppressed bad feelings by keeping themselves engaged by reading books and focusing on work. In an important way, these everyday distractions open up a space for Rohingya women to take control of their lives. Despite the hardship of living in the camps, these daily routines – the 'repeated actions, those most travelled journeys, those most inhabited spaces that make up, literally, the day to day' (Highmore 2011: 1) – make the camps feel like 'home'.

Part of the 'home-making' process also entails cementing bonds with those who share similar experiences of exile, despite the lack of prior personal connection. These new community bonds provide a source of friendship, company, and support in the camps. The significant reduction in private space in the camps also reduced opportunities to engage privately in domestic activities such as cooking and food preparation. However, food preparation has now become a community event – often, women sit outside together on the front steps of their shelters cleaning and cutting vegetables, providing an opportunity to bond with other women. These newly forged social ties become especially important for parenting, as women come to rely on other women in their vicinity to help look after their children. Because of the higher proportion of men killed by the Burmese army, women outnumber men in the camp and thus carry a particularly high burden in ensuring that children are taken care of, as they may be the only parent of a child. Zolekha noted the importance of community support in helping to raise her young children in the absence of family members.

> In our village in Myanmar we had all our family members and the women used to take care of the children. The men would do the work, but now that my husband died I have to go to pick up food in the bazaar or pick up wood for cooking. I worry about my babies because I cannot carry them in the heat and walk so long to get the items. But at least I am relieved to have the support of my neighbours who look after my children when I have to go out.

Rohingya women are thus able to create a sense of belonging by developing daily routines that help infuse the camp with intimate meanings by forging new social ties with immediate community members based on common daily activities and shared experiences of exile. Another specific way in which Rohingya women have been able to maintain past traditions and recover a sense of self is through participation in *taleem*s, which have become an important space of solace, belonging, and a space to reclaim subjectivity – a replica of a custom held in Myanmar that continues to operate in Bangladesh's refugee camps.

Transformative Ties

The Taleem: A Sanctuary

Within Bangladesh's sprawling refugee camps, humanitarian aid and development organizations have set up a number of 'women-friendly spaces' and 'multi-purpose women's centers' with the aim of providing a safe environment where women and girls can access awareness sessions on gender-based violence and mental health support, amongst other services. While these spaces have all proven to be important for advancing Rohingya women's access to resources, throughout the course of my fieldwork, however, I found that a significant portion of Rohingya women in the camps are not making use of these NGO-run initiatives. For my interlocutors, the *taleem* provides both a space that evokes memories of positive experiences and a sense of belonging, safety, and hope in the midst of tremendous trauma.

Taleem – literally meaning 'education' in Arabic – is a common word used by groups in South Asia referring to gatherings of prayer and supplication. These gatherings are supplementary and not part of the obligatory prayers in Islam. I visited a few *taleem*s in various parts of the Balukhali camp, which are commonly held every week. *Taleem*s take place mostly on Fridays after Jumu'ah (Friday-afternoon congregational prayer), though they can take place on other days as well, depending on the availability of space in one of the women's shelters. Throughout my fieldwork, mention of *taleem*s came up frequently during my discussions with women I met at the camp, many often asking one another whether they would be attending an upcoming session, and some always inviting me to participate. It became clear to me that, for many Rohingya women, *taleem*s are a very big part of their lives in Bangladesh's refugee camps.

Quiet Bonds

It was a sunny Friday afternoon in late June 2018 as Munni and I walked past rows of shelters. By now, we had already been walking for 40 minutes through the maze-like narrow pathways in the Balukhali camp. The Jumu'ah prayer had just ended, and the relentless sunrays provided little afternoon solace. In the distance, I could see a group of men hurrying out of a makeshift mosque at the bottom of the hill. Fridays mark the start of the weekend in Bangladesh and so activity in the camp was low, and the heat of the afternoon sun meant most people were resting indoors. Munni and I were making our way to the *taleem* that was being held at the shelters of one of my interlocutors, Zomila.

At the end of a narrow bend at the top of the hillside, wearing a long pink shawl pulled over her head and upper body and a flowery printed *bazu*, 35-year-old Zomila met us at the door of her shelter. It was my second time attending the *taleem* in Zomila's shelter. Zomila was seen as somewhat of a leader in the community – she lived with her elderly mother and brother. Without a husband and children, and as her brother usually remained outdoors for the whole day, she was keen to hold the *taleem* in her shelter. We stepped inside, and she led me through a stained cream curtain that acted as a partition from the 'living room' space where 13 women (some with babies on their laps) and young girls sat on straw mats on the dusty mud floor – some quietly waiting, others chattering to one another in hushed voices. A few other women slowly entered the large, open room until every space on the floor was occupied. I had met some of the women during my previous visits to the *taleem*, and we all exchanged greetings with one another – 'salaam alaykum' (peace be upon you), handshakes, and hugs. There were still a few more minutes before the *alima* (learned person, or teacher) would arrive and the lesson would begin, so the quiet chatter continued amongst each other.

Many of the women waited quietly, fiddling with their long shawls and scarves or tending to their children. The conversations in the group that did take place were hushed and subdued, often discussing daily activities or some interesting news of the day. One woman read softly from the Qur'an on a *rehal* (book rest) perched on their lap as others listened beside her. I sat next to Aleya, who was watching the activity around her but not saying a word. Like many of the Rohingya women I met at the camp, Aleya brought with her harrowing experiences of torture and rape in Myanmar and losing her unborn child on the difficult journey to Bangladesh. She now lives with her elderly mother, older brother, and two-year-old daughter; her husband and father were killed by the Mog. She told me that she often liked to sit in silence in the moments before the *alima* arrived and began her *taleem*. She said:

> I lost many of my family members in Myanmar so I don't know many people here in the camp except those who live in the shelters next to mine, like Zomila. I am always worried about what will happen with our lives and our future. That's why I like coming here [the *taleem*]. I am okay to just be quiet and listen to others recite the Qur'an, and I want to always learn more from the *alima*. That is most important to me. I don't like to share my *dukkho* [sadness] – nobody here likes to. Everyone ... all of us Rohingyas have bad memories; it is not our way to talk about these memories with each other. For me, just sitting with the other women and hearing Allah's words makes me feel safe and I feel that I am part of a community. That's why I keep coming back every time.

Aleya's narrative of finding the *taleem* to be a 'safe' space and feeling of 'togetherness' resonated with many of the other Rohingya women who attend them. Having a safe space is essential in creating a 'restorative' experience for refugees (Sampson and Gifford 2010). Aleya's preference for camaraderie and religious knowledge over recollecting experiences of grief was a common sentiment amongst the women at the *taleem*. All of the women present at the *taleem* possess the tacit knowledge that each person has experienced tremendous suffering, and they all find support in their mutual quest to move forward, day to day. The most powerful support thus surrounded that which was unsaid – the creation of a safe space where women could personally deal with their individual trauma while drawing support from the simple presence of others. I found that the feeling of being part of a 'community' extended to powerful notions of friendship and bonds through the shared, collective prayer space of the *taleem*. It became a site for Rohingya women to forge friendships and bonds through a common spiritual goal. One of my interlocutors, Amena, whom I met at a larger *taleem* of about 20 women also in the Balukhali camp, passionately told me:

> We must come here [to the *taleem*]! Today is Jumu'ah – it is a blessed day. *Allah'r laak laak shokr* [lots of thanks to Allah] that we are here together. This is an even bigger blessing. We are given this opportunity to be grateful to the One who has kept us safe. In my free time I only read Qur'an and make lots of *du'a* [supplication]. My favourite part of the week is when I come here – I get to see my friends and pray with them. Did you know there is even more blessings when you make *du'a* together in a group?

As we spoke, Amena's friend Sharifa added: 'We have nowhere to go now. We only have Allah and each other.'

Aleya, Amena, and Sharifa's feelings of being part of a 'community' and finding friendship with other women in the *taleem* are significant in the way they are able to create a sense of belonging. They look forward to coming to the *taleem* and the space it provides to share moments with others, which makes them want to keep returning. In many ways, the *taleem* necessitates and facilitates bonds and friendships. In her research with Palestinian refugees living in camps in Lebanon, Maria Holt (2015) notes how the women she spoke to derived 'strength' from staying together and supporting each other. For Rohingya women, despite not necessarily speaking to each other while attending the *taleem*, the moments of collective silence and shared prayer are powerful – showing unity and strength, and in essence, a sense of belonging is created. Coming together in this manner provides a 'social support network' for these women (Khawaja et al. 2008). Beyond simply providing a space for prayer, Rohingya women's attachment to the *taleem* is revealed and preserved by the social relations they encounter within the space, giving it meaning and allowing them to actively feel like they belong within a 'community' (Kawachi and Berkman 2001).

Relief in Prayer

The activities of the *taleem* officially begin once the *alima* arrives and everyone settles down. The session starts off with a group *dhikr* (remembrance of God by reciting short prayers) led by the *alima* and everyone joining in, lasting for about 15 minutes. Then the *alima* begins the lesson. It is commonplace during this time that everyone sits in concentric circles around the *alima*. The *alima's* eyes had a certain depth to them, and all of the women carried themselves with a heightened sense of humility in her presence. The *alima* beautifully recites from the Qur'an – first reading the Arabic with a musical tone and then going on to read and explain the translation in the Rohingya language. Time is spent reflecting on the meanings, which for many Rohingya women is an important part of maintaining their spirituality, as Amena told me:

> It is so important to understand what we are reading. We don't understand the Arabic so that's why I come to learn here. The *alima* gives the translation and explains it for us. When she tells us the meaning I reflect on it. It helps me to stay calm when I start getting stressed about my situation. I can't deal with all these worries sometimes. I need something to keep me calm.

Religious observance and belief in God as a coping strategy have received some attention in literature on refugee populations (Shoeb, Weinstein, and Halpern 2007; Khawaja et al. 2008; Matheson, Jorden, and Anisman 2008). Religious coping strategies have been described as 'motivated by a search for meaning, intimacy and self' and give Rohingya women a place of belonging within this 'spiritual space' (Shoeb, Weinstein, and Halpern 2007). For women like Amena, the *taleem* both symbolizes a spiritual haven and serves as a space through which she can process and deal with her worries and stress. During my time attending *taleem*s, it was clear that the meaningful and restorative nature of the *taleem* provided Rohingya women a space in which to cope and heal (Sampson and Gifford 2010). After at least an hour (sometimes more) of lessons, and of the women listening, learning, and reflecting on the teachings, the session then turns to reciting *du'a*s (supplication). When I attended the *taleem* at Zomila's home that hot summer day in June, it was no different. After the lesson, the *alima* first began by making a *du'a* in solitude and then reciting it aloud. She then asked the group to face towards the *qibla* (the direction of Mecca) and raise their hands as she began the collective *du'a*. As the *du'a*s were recited, tears streamed endlessly on the faces of all the women present – some cried softly, their faces dug deep into their shawls that covered their raised hands; others raised their voices in prayer and loud cries. Prayers and crying thus became therapeutic. Ayesha (introduced in Chapter 3) had attended the *taleem* for the first time after Zomila invited her to join a few months prior. She shared with me how coming to this space had been a transformative experience for her as she struggled through traumatic memories of rape and losing all three of her children – two of whom were killed during the violence in Myanmar; she lost the third baby she was pregnant with during the journey to Bangladesh. She spoke softly, holding back tears:

> I could not live. Sometimes I stayed up all night crying and asking Allah to take me away. I wake up in the middle in the night and sit for hours staring into the darkness. I was praying and praying but I was suffering inside. I kept thinking of what happened and felt angry, sad, frustrated – I wanted to kill myself. I wanted my children to come back. [*There is silence for a few minutes as tears stream down her cheeks.*] I didn't know who to turn to or where to go. And then I heard about the *taleem*s and went to it in Zomila's place. *Allah'r shokr*, it helped me a lot. When I cry by myself so many bad thoughts come to my mind. But then in the *taleem* everyone is crying together – like all of our worries are coming out together. It makes me feel a thousand times better, as though a big weight is lifted from my heart. I had no will to live. But look at me now – I am surviving.

As *du'a*s are made, the tears flow endlessly, and time is temporarily forgotten. The duration of the supplication can last from at least one hour and in some cases up to a few hours until '*Asr* (late afternoon) prayer. 'We like to make *du'a* for a long time. It is such a blessed time, especially on Jumu'ah day. The more *du'a* we can make, the more we can ask Allah to relieve our pain and sorrow', Zomila would tell me. Talking about the time of supplication and its meaning to her, Ayesha further shared with me, as she looked off into the distance at nothing in particular, with a sad smile on her face:

> Making *du'a* together and crying gives me relief, even if only for a short time. In that short time, I feel like there is hope and I can forget all my worries. When we make *du'a* it means that we leave all our worries with Allah, and for those few moments I feel that there is no more pain and no more suffering and no more bad memories.

Ayesha's words were deeply poignant – they reminded me of the value of spaces like the *taleem* that offered women a haven to unburden themselves from the trauma of the past, even if temporarily. For Rohingya women, being in the *taleem* and engaging in collective prayer become an important part of the healing and coping process. This 'momentary relief', as Ayesha so eloquently described, and her feelings of having a 'big weight lifted' by attending the *taleem* are important in understanding how prayer – and the space for collective prayer – is significant in Rohingya women's placemaking strategies in the refugee camps. Placemaking and giving meaning to places play an important role in the coping process for refugees, through what can be seen as a 'therapeutic landscape', to decrease feelings of sadness, distress, and traumatic memories (Sampson and Gifford 2010). For women like Ayesha, while it is clear that the act of prayer is a central part of the coping process, the act of coming together to collectively pray in a group setting in a way creates a 'new space of belonging' that works to heal and restore their lives.

Memories of Home

The *taleem* at Zomila's shelter ended once the *alima* finished the supplication – not a dry eye remained in the room. The heat of the afternoon summer sun made the room increasingly stuffy, and so once she finished her *du'a*, Zomila quickly drew open the curtain in the middle of the room to allow air to flow in. Some women lingered on a while longer, praying a little bit more on their own; others sat in quiet solitude. A few of the women began to quickly disperse out of the space and into the late afternoon sun to carry on with their daily activities, hurrying along with their children in their arms. I noticed that one of my interlocutors, 22-year-old Ismat Ara, walked up to shake my hand and say her goodbye *salaam* before quickly rushing off with her 1-year-old son.

I later met Ismat Ara in her shelter one day, and we spoke at length on many topics, mostly regarding her life in Myanmar, the arduous journey to Bangladesh, and her family. The topic of her husband came up – whom she had married in June 2017, right before the mass exodus, when she arrived in September at the camps with him. During our conversation about her marriage, she asked me about my own marriage and was curious to know more. I shared, and we discussed it at length. At one point, Ismat Ara stopped speaking and did not say anything for a few moments before blurting out: 'Do you know why I always leave so quickly from the *taleem*?' she asked me. Before I could say anything, she continued:

I go there [to the *taleem*] as early as possible, but I have to leave quickly because I know my husband does not like for me to stay on longer than necessary. So, I go home as fast as possible. My husband does not let me go anywhere. But I told him I have to go to the *taleem* because it is only for women and we are doing religious things. You know, we used to have *taleem* in Burma? It reminds me of better times in Burma. When I sit here [in the shelter] I feel depressed – this is not a home, it is only a box made out of bamboo and tarp. It is hard for us Rohingya women – we don't have any opportunities and nothing to do here in the camp.

Ismat Ara's stirring narrative reveals an important aspect of the connection to the *taleem*. It is clear that the 'gendering of place relates to feeling at home' (Moghissi 1999; Sampson and Gifford 2010: 117). Due to cultural practices of gender segregation in the Rohingya community, women are more often relegated to spaces in the home, and movement around the camp is often limited. Thus, the *taleem* is seen to be a space exclusively for women, such that even Ismat Ara's husband allowed her to attend only because no men would be present. Furthermore, for Ismat Ara, not having a 'home', but rather only having a shelter – a dwelling made out of bamboo and tarp – the physical space of the *taleem* does not so much provide a sense of 'home', but rather it is the 'personal dimension' that gives meaning to it (Turton 2005; Cross 2015).

There was an overwhelming feeling of comfort amongst the women who attended the *taleem*s. This 'temporary space' Rohingya women created provided a momentary microcosm of a home that once was, as Zomila powerfully articulated, the evening after the *taleem* in her shelter ended and as I helped her tidy up the room, rolling some of the bamboo mats and putting them away:

I hope you are enjoying the *taleem* with us. [*She continued before I could reply.*] In your book you must write that I really wanted to hold it here because in Burma we used to have these gatherings. I know other areas here in the camps are also doing it. I informed the *majhee* about it and set it up. I felt it was important to have something like this here in the camps. When I was growing up, in our house in our village in Burma my mother used to hold *taleem*s. It was just a few people – the women in my family that lived with us – me, my mother, my sisters, aunt, and a few female cousins. [*She held my hand and began crying.*] Though we have experienced so much suffering and pain, when I think of those memories now I still look back fondly. My heart aches for my village. This gathering I hold here is just a small reminder of those happy times when my whole family used to be together – us girls we used to laugh, pray, and have lots of fun together. [*She was uncontrollably crying now, using her pink shawl to wipe her tears.*] It's not the same here, but I am trying my best. I take pride in knowing I can hold the *taleem* for us [Rohingya women]. I have nothing left. So, I try to do small things to take control of my life in a place where I don't have anything. Holding this *taleem* in one of my small efforts.

Zomila's words were a poignant revelation of the deep emotional, cognitive, and psychological attachment to a space like the *taleem* (Scannell and Gifford 2010). The place attachment to the *taleem* for Rohingya women like Zomila evokes positive memories of life in Myanmar – the nostalgia they remember for the 'happy times' is closely attached to the bond they hold to the *taleem*. Similarly, the act of trying to replicate such a space in displacement is a deliberate attempt at placemaking, to maintain 'a link with a place [that] provides a sense of continuity to a person's identity' (Twigger-Ross and Uzell 1996). Rohingya women's identity is strongly attached to the *taleem* – it was always a gendered space in Myanmar, reserved exclusively for women; to be able to replicate that in displacement is significant (Hartsock 1983). Ultimately, these feelings evolve out of the complex, dynamic experience of a home lost (in Myanmar) but also a sense of belonging preserved (in the *taleem*) through their collective organizing (Gren 2015).

The *taleem* had thus become a way to re-establish the social structures of lost communities and a way of bringing together dispersed lives through the shared customs of prayer and remembrance. For Rohingya women, it plays an important role in forging a sense of belonging in displacement.

*

Research on the *taleem* at the Rohingya refugee camps in Bangladesh reveals the significance of such spaces for Rohingya women as a semblance of home, hope, and well-being. Although the harrowing experiences of forced migration and displacement can lead to a loss of identity and social belonging for Rohingya women, the *taleem* creates a spiritual, psychological, and emotional haven that allows for bonds and friendships to emerge. The act of collective prayer and recreating an experiential space that evokes positive emotions of 'home' is a significant part of the healing and coping process. Given the traumatic nature of forced migration, my interlocutors identify and actively contribute towards this placemaking endeavour to gain a sense of belonging in their everyday life (Seamon 2014).

In this manner, it is what Turton (2005) suggests are the efforts made towards – and possibilities in – creating connections and meanings to new sites, despite profound loss. It is a space, as Clifford Geertz (2000: 17) notes, where humans live 'suspended in webs of meaning they themselves have spun' and continue to spin. Through these efforts, my interlocutors recreate new meanings and gendered roles and expectations for themselves; their subjective sense of self is thus remoulded in relation to these changed meanings (Merry 2006a, 2006b). The new affective ties Rohingya women create with other women in the *taleem* allow for the transformation of their gendered self. Gay Becker's (1994: 4) assertion is particularly relevant: 'Restoring order to life necessitates reworking understandings of the self and the world, redefining the disruption and life itself.'

Conclusion

The settling-in process for Rohingya refugees once they arrived at the camps was somewhat haphazard, with various challenges associated with locating family that were lost on the journey to Bangladesh, coming to terms with new notions of 'community' after exile, and renewing and transforming their sense of belonging. Loss of family and the support systems of relatives, friends, and neighbours, which once were an integral part of village life in Myanmar, deeply affected Rohingya women's gendered subjectivities. My interlocutors' gendered *sense of self* was usually tied to the wider web of social relations they were part of. Losing those critical ties often led to deep isolation. With time, the meaning of 'home' and belonging evolved, now encompassing those who lived around their shelters – their neighbours and other distant kin. These ties and bonds become an important part of the home-making experience during times of uncertainty after displacement.

Ethnographic research on the *taleem* at the Rohingya refugee camps in Bangladesh reveals its significance for Rohingya women as it provides a semblance of home, hope, and well-being. Although the harrowing experiences of forced migration and displacement can lead to a loss of identity and social belonging for Rohingya women, the *taleem* creates a spiritual, psychological, and emotional haven that allows for new bonds and friendships to emerge. The act of collective prayer and recreating an experiential space that has a meaningful and restorative nature through religious observance is a significant part of the healing and coping process. Given the traumatic nature of forced migration, Rohingya women identify and actively contribute towards this placemaking endeavour that evokes positive emotions of 'home' to gain a sense of belonging in their everyday life.

Beyond Brides
On Marriage and Moral Panics

Karima's Wedding

Preparations for Karima's wedding to Hossain were under way. It was Thursday afternoon in April 2018 and the narrow alleyway in this part of the Balukhali camp – 2 miles away from the entrance of the camp – was teeming with life and excitement. The wedding was only a few hours away, *baad 'Asr* (after the late afternoon prayer). Eighteen-year-old Karima was in her shelter with her future sister-in-law, niece, and other relatives who had gathered to watch the bride prepare for her big day. Strings of artificial orange and pink flowers hung all around the room. Karima's hands had decorative floral patterns inked in *mehndi* (henna) the night before, and she sat patiently as her sister-in-law applied makeup and lipstick. A strikingly red scarf was adorned on her head and also covered some of her face. As I headed outside to see what the men were up to during this time, I noticed two young girls peeking their heads and giggling through the door of Karima's shelter. I stopped to chat with them and inquired what they thought of the wedding taking place. 'Did you know they met in the camp?! How lucky she is!', one of the girls exclaimed, covering her mouth as she giggled. Karima's male relative, who was walking by, shouted at the girls upon hearing them: 'Hey! Speak quietly about these things!'. The girls hid their faces with their scarves and quickly darted off.

Outside the shelter, the men of Karima's family and community gathered around the *huzur* (local religious leader), who sat with Karima's father and uncles to negotiate the *mahr* (Islamic gift to the bride from the groom) and dowry (from the bride to the groom). The *majhee* was also present to ensure that everything was running smoothly. After a few minutes of back-and-forth between the male relatives of the bride and groom, the atmosphere started getting tense. The discussion became increasingly dotted with minor shouting outbursts as both sides made demands about the marriage. At one point, Karima's father shouted: 'Nothing has happened with her and Hossain!

My daughter is pure and no *zulm* has ever happened to her. She must get a *mahr*. In fact, her *mahr* should be increased because of Hossain's interest!' In response, Hossain's relatives snapped back: 'You should feel lucky that Hossain is marrying your daughter given the situation we have here. Nobody pays *mahr* anymore.' The disagreement continued for a while as the *huzur* and *majhee* worked to settle the concerns. Eventually, a small white cloth filled with gold jewellery and other ornaments was handed over from the groom's uncle to the bride's father. At this point, the harsh crease on the bride's father's face immediately softened, and with a welcoming tone, he quickly promised a large sum of money for the groom, which would be paid shortly before the wedding took place. As this exchange was completed outside, one lady excitedly rushed indoors, where the women were getting ready to announce that the *akth* (solemnization of marriage; signing of the marriage contract) would begin shortly.

*

The intense agony of war and forced migration is often associated with the fracturing of social norms and practices that had previously constituted everyday life. Such narratives fail to account for the ways in which these experiences of violence and rupture, as well as previously held traditions, both play a role in shaping new understandings of daily life and the choices made by those navigating a new world. Like other parts of one's identity, gender identities travel with a refugee from setting to setting, transforming at each point in response to varying stimuli in the new environment while still maintaining a link with the past. Such transformations in gender identity take place in a refugee camp. This process of transformation, negotiation, and remoulding results in a set of social norms and practices that neither reproduces the past nor renounces it in full but rather recasts it in the new environment – and the extreme pressures of the refugee camp are no exception.

Laura Hammond (2004), in her research on Eritrean refugees in Kenya, found that one of the signs of life slowly progressing and 'returning to normal' in the refugee camp was the increasing frequency of marriages taking place. Within the Rohingya refugee camps, marriage and the process of marriage – relationships, socializing, weddings, and so on – are a central component of Rohingya social reproduction. Marriage recreates the bonds of family that may have been lost or damaged during violence and migration. In the months following exile, the slow process of *living* – not simply *surviving* – begins to unfold. Research conducted in refugee situations has examined changing gender relationships but only rarely focuses on the ways in which such relationships play out in the course of routine life. The focus often remains on issues with immediate policy relevance, such as sexual exploitation and gender violence. More often neglected are the dynamics of 'normal' life in the camps and the goals, aspirations, and dreams of refugees. Rather than arguing that social norms, culture, family, and gender roles are irrevocably changed through war and displacement – whether by adopting more liberal or more conservative practices in the new setting – I instead explore the ways in which Rohingya women are negotiating their future, their relationships, and their families – often in an unanticipated manner.

Systems of kinship and marriage always entail compromises between the different interests of men and women in various relationships (Bourdieu 1977). The power balance in these systems is delicate and can be overturned quite easily by changes in economic, social, or political conditions. A gendered analysis offers new insights into the challenges and consequences of forced migration for men and women and their relationships with each other, their families, and their children. Normative expectations regarding the responsibilities and 'proper' behaviour of women and men and the suitability of certain relationships are renegotiated in a new context. This chapter is thus guided by the following questions: What are the kinds of relationships that exist in the camp setting? Are Rohingya marriage norms evolving in the camps? Ambivalence surrounds conjugal relationships in the camp and the competing notions of what a marriage entails: Is it a relationship negotiated between two people, is it a family-arranged affair, or is it a partnership born out of necessity? What are the 'new' gendered identities with regard to marriage that have developed, and how are women navigating them? In this chapter, I look at the ways in which marriage is viewed by Rohingya women by focusing on the renegotiations of self, gender identities, and aspirations. I predominantly focus on the experiences of young women and their families, as their insights, emotions, and experiences shed light on how gender identities regarding marriage are transforming in the camp. In the next chapter, I expand this analysis by looking at the ways in which power plays a role within the family, particularly through the lens of gender divisions of labour.

The Rohingya Marriage Process

I sat with Ahmed and Momtaz Khatun – husband and wife – whom I often visited in their shelter in a narrow alleyway in Balukhali camp close to their shop. Their son and son-in-law were murdered by the Mog in Myanmar, and their elder daughter – who was pregnant at the time – was raped by the

Myanmar army, though she initially survived. However, upon arriving at the camps in Bangladesh, the elder daughter died during childbirth along with the baby. While the couple were slowly getting by and rebuilding a life for themselves with the knowledge that a return to Myanmar in the foreseeable future was unlikely, these days their eyes were filled with worry about their only remaining child, 23-year-old Khushida, who was of marriageable age. Life as a refugee was difficult, and the prospects of marriage were dim as family structures had scarcely weathered the storms of conflict and flight from Myanmar. As we spoke, they told me that marriage was the most important part of a Rohingya woman's life. Momtaz first told me of her own marriage 20 years prior, when the situation in Myanmar was 'a bit better those days than now'. They were both from Buthidaung township – she was 18 at the time, and Ahmed was 19. They were cousins on their father's side, and their respective fathers had agreed to their marriage at birth. It was the happiest day of her life, she tells me. Though she was young, she told me of how her mother had prepared her for marriage since she was 10, explaining that it was a woman's responsibility to marry, take care of her husband, have children, and raise a family of her own. Now, more than 20 years later, Momtaz is worried that the time for Khushida is passing her by. She solemnly told me:

> You know in our culture for us, marriage is very important and it is arranged by the parents. Especially the marriage of a girl at the right time. We have suffered so much in Myanmar … [*she trailed off*] … but never mind, we are here now. At least we have somewhere to live. So now we have to think of the future of our children. Khushida is getting old. At this age we expected our daughters to be married to continue our family. We need to have grandchildren. I don't know how long we will survive this, so my only *du'a* now is that she gets married quickly and I can see the faces of my grandchildren before my last breath.

Momtaz's account highlights the significance of marriage in the social reproduction of family and lineage in the Rohingya community. Especially due to the precariousness of life in the refugee camps, 'marriages and starting of one's own household were linked to the (re)creation of social networks' (Grabska 2014: 305). For women like Khushida, there is a general expectation that she will follow the process of getting married in a similar way to her parents and most Rohingyas – a spouse will be found for her. As Momtaz noted, 'That's what happened to me – there was not much choice in the matter. We will do the same for Khushida.' Her remarks parallel the research of Rosemary Sayigh (2002: 323), whose work with Palestinian women in Lebanon's refugee camps found that

the primary institution of control of women is marriage, which was practically
obligatory in camps and always subject to parental agreement. Marriage controls
women beforehand through the importance attached to virginity and afterwards
through the responsibilities of childbearing and housework, and the many kinds
of social labor attached to the housewife role.

For Momtaz, marriage was a focal point in her own life, shaping her
upbringing and subsequent role as a mother; similarly, she viewed marriage as
a central component of her daughter's life as it would define her place within
the community.

In the Rohingya camps, the relationships associated with marriage reveal a
continuum that reflects the salience of gender, life course stage, and the status
of future plans. It is in exploring the significance of these relationships that
we gain insight into counter-narratives that contradict the view of refugees
as being devoid of agency. In the sections that follow, I detail the ways in
which gender identity is negotiated through the marriage process in the
camps by focusing on the candid – and sometimes contradictory – insights
of my interlocutors, who are themselves navigating transforming practices
and expectations within a new environment. My focus is on the everyday,
mundane aspects of getting married for Rohingya women and the freedoms
and constraints that marriage entails.

Freedoms and Frustrations

Marriage was certainly on the minds of young women like Khushida.
In women's gatherings inside and outside shacks, women would giggle, dream,
and hope about what the future held, particularly when it came to marriage.
The importance of marriage was widely discussed amongst my young female
interlocutors. One afternoon, I was with Khushida and a few of her friends in
Khushida's shelter when 19-year-old Zannat walked in with her younger sister
Sajeda. Zannat arrived in the camps one year prior; her mother died many
years earlier during childbirth, so now it was her father, two brothers, and
younger sister with her. 'Here comes the beauty queen!' Khushida remarked
winking at Zannat. 'We are sure she will get married very soon – she is so
desperate to get married, we are all praying that it will happen, *inshaAllah*
[God willing].' The girls all laughed, including Zannat. I asked Zannat
why she was 'desperate' for marriage and what being married meant for her.
She enthusiastically replied:

Afa ... I have always been ready for *biya-shaadi* [marriage]! [*She laughed out loud wholeheartedly; we all laughed along*] ... It is hard to find a husband these days as you know because we lost everything in the war but we still have hopes and dreams. And I always dreamt of being a married woman since I was a little girl. Think of how much *azadi* [freedom] you have when you get married. It will give a new happiness in life. We will still be in this camp but at least there will be love and the start of something new.

The concept of marriage as 'freedom' and the ability to 'create a new life' was something I heard regularly amongst the young women that I met (Grabska 2014; Grønlund 2016; Taha 2019). Many felt that after experiencing immense suffering and loss, a sense of stability was finally starting to settle in the camps, and the prospects of marriage provided hope for the future. Another woman, Hajera, echoed Zannat's statement:

We want to live our own lives and do all the things that women do. In Burma we were stuck with so many family responsibilities but now there is hope for me to start fresh in a new phase of life. Thinking of marriage gives me something to look forward to. I will have children and they will keep me busy.

For young women like Zannat and Hajera, marriage provides a renewed sense of hope that had been missing due to the overwhelming suffering they had faced during the process of forced migration. Their narratives reveal that marriage would not only give *azadi* but also respect. For Hajera, marriage is associated with having children, which affords a woman status given her role in the social reproduction of the community. Christine Grønlund (2016: 52) notes that after arriving in refugee camps, women see it as a 'relief to finally be able to marry and start families, and that it is good to have family and children to spend time with in daily life' as a way to 'continue' with their lives, hope for a more positive future, and re-establish their status within the community. Grabska (2014), in her research, found that South Sudanese returnee girls viewed marriage and procreation as a passage to 'womanhood' that subsequently increased social positioning. Social positioning was important in gaining respect within the community and not being viewed as a 'young girl' (Radhakrishnan 2009; Vera-Sanso 2016). For Rohingya women, marriage was viewed as a way to increase their social status, which in turn granted them greater independence. Marriage thus served as a marker of their gender identity, providing girls a passage into womanhood and affording women greater independence because of the respect for their new status within the community.

Some of my interlocutors, however, were quick to point out the downsides and constraints of marriage, especially within the camps. Throughout our conversations, it was clear that the new setting of the camp, in contrast to life in Myanmar, opened up the possibility of new ways of thinking about marriage. Many women were exposed to the possibility of learning skills and participating in trainings offered by NGOs operating in the camps and were weary of what marriage would do for their 'dreams' of being able to utilize these new skills. Despite severe restrictions in the camp with regard to mobility and lack of education, some young women worried that getting married at a young age would reduce their chances of receiving an education and restrict their ability to develop their skills through the new opportunities available to them. I was with Shofika one evening on the doorstep of her shelter as we ate peanuts, and she spoke deeply about marriage, confiding in me her pain from the past and the frustration for her future. Her brother Kobir had recently suggested Shofika get married to a friend he made in the camp, but Shofika was not interested. Before most of her family had been killed in Myanmar, her father had taught her to read at a very basic level and wanted her to get an education if circumstances permitted. On this topic, she remarked:

> I think of marriage sometimes because I know now is the time to for me to settle down. But we have just arrived in this new country. I just started volunteering at a children-friendly space two days a week with one NGO – who knows what other opportunities will open up for me, *inshaAllah*. My brother is trying to set me up with one of his friends and telling me that it is the correct next step for me. My *khala* keeps telling me that it will be better for me to start my own life and move forward because life for an *abiyata mayya-fua* (unmarried girl) is always difficult. [*She pauses to look out at the horizon, her hand picking up and dropping the sand at her feet*] If my *Abba* was still alive he would tell me to get married but he would also support my dreams. He would want me to get married to someone who will help me get an education, find a job, and think about my future – not be stuck in a marriage.

Shofika's narrative reveals the difficult negotiations young women in the camps experience as they worry about what their future holds and the constraints that marriage may entail. Her exposure to learning and the possibility of gaining an education in her youth, coupled with her experiences as a volunteer, have exposed her to broader ideas of what could be possible for her and her future. The prospects of being 'stuck' in a marriage could mean that such opportunities would no longer be possible, thereby restricting her freedom. Shofika's predicament highlights the question of power and control with regard to social structures and relations. It speaks to a concept put forth by Sherry Ortner (1996: 12), that of 'serious games', focusing on resistance and transformation within society not as 'autonomous agents', but rather as people embodying agency full of 'skill, intention, and intelligence'. Shofika went on to explain that part of why she was opposed to her brother's offer was also due to his insistence that her marriage and subsequent departure from the home would mean one less mouth to feed in their shelter. The difficulties for men in securing employment in the camps (detailed in the next chapter, which discusses the gender divisions of labour and gender livelihoods), mean that families are often eager to get their daughters or sisters married as quickly as possible so that their financial responsibilities will fall on their husbands.

For Shofika, despite being in a clearly complicated position, she worked to navigate the multiple expectations, constraints, and desires that come with the discussion of marriage, especially in a culture where men (such as fathers, brothers, husbands, and so on) largely make the decisions on such matters for the women in their lives. Unlike Zannat, Shofika did not view marriage as giving her 'freedom', but instead as doing the exact opposite. Shofika's narrative illustrates her strategic use of her learned background to find a balance between her education and her own choice of husband; she herself wanted to go beyond the 'respectable femininity' that is deeply engrained in Rohingya culture (Radhakrishnan 2009: 199). She went on to tell me:

> I know life is hard here and it is impossible to find a job and secure an employment. I do want to get married, but is it bad if I want to marry someone who at least tries to do honest work? Many of our Rohingya men do not know how to even write their name – that is not their fault, I'm not saying that – our situation was so bad in Myanmar there was no opportunities for them. I can read and write – I want someone who can at least do that much, because then he will be more open to me continuing my volunteer work and eventually finding a job. But my brother says it is hard to find someone like that in the camps and he does not listen to what I want. He says I am too picky and stubborn and says that my *matha haraf hoye* [gone crazy; literally: the brain is not working]. He says that if I don't get married, I will ruin the *izzot* [honour or social reputation] of the family. Everyone is always concerned about *izzot* in our culture. For now, I am trying my best to delay getting married.

It is important to touch on the concept of *izzot* in Rohingya culture, which was regularly mentioned by my interlocutors. *Izzot* is the primary social norm governing Rohingya women's actions and is at the core of how Rohingya women are often made to uphold traditional cultural values.

In their consultations with Rohingyas in the refugee camps, Daniel Coyle and Mohammed Abdullah Jainul (2020: 12) note that *izzot* 'plays an anchoring role for Rohingya' and is defined through adherence to religious and social norms as a value system, governing the social reputations of men and women in Rohingya society. As such, as Shofika's narratives suggest, there is a constant desire to uphold the dignity and *izzot* of one's family, especially by being an upright daughter, which is continually at odds with the very real desires for education and pursuing personal aspirations.

Marriage was thus seen as simultaneously a freeing and constraining act within the circumstances of life in the camps, and it was constantly a process to negotiate gender identities and relations, but it was still a necessary part of life in the minds of my interlocutors. Marriage is an important part of Rohingya social reproduction and a way to recreate and re-establish 'the landscape of social relations that gave a meaning to the everyday actions and interactions' (Grabska 2014: 321). All these negotiations and diverse practices of reshaping gender identities still point to the fact that, despite the difficulties of the refugee experience, Rohingya women still see marriage as the way to move on and forward with their lives (Gale 2006).

Surveilling Youth and Maintaining *Izzot*

I noticed quite quickly that there were changing notions of love and intimacy in relation to marriage against the larger backdrop of 'moral panics' in the camps. 'Love marriage' and 'affairs' – that is, being in a relationship before marriage – were becoming increasingly prevalent in the refugee camp. Kazi Fahmida Farzana (2017: 156) notes that despite parents playing a central role in the lives of their children with regard to marriage, 'nowadays, it is not unusual to discover refugees having affairs'. I heard stories of how family pressure drove girls and young women to 'do it in their own way', as mentioned by Khushida. Young women, in navigating perceptions of selfhood with regard to love and marriage, are more often than not up against a series of moral panics within the camps, particularly due to the close quarters of the shelters. The method of tent distribution, and the configuration of the shelter itself, has led to shifts in household social structures. Privacy and security become important matters since shelters cannot be closed properly or locked – a flimsy bamboo and straw entrance must suffice as a door which often opens directly onto busy, narrow walkways.

Holly Porter (2020: 12), in her research on Ugandan refugees' intimate lives, notes that 'close quarters made contact with strangers more common and made the oversight of children and youth by elders nearly impossible'. This caused elders, parents, and other community leaders to be extra attentive about the goings-on of their children's intimate lives and relationships. And as such, life remains exposed and susceptible to external intrusions. During my time in the Rohingya refugee camps, I noticed that families and elders became increasingly worried that traditional restrictions on taboos, such as the mixing of men and women – especially those who are young and unmarried – could not be maintained in the same way as in their villages back in Myanmar, and thus families feared that the youth may indulge in sexual activities in violation of village and religious traditions, or choose spouses on their own without consideration for cultural norms and expectations. This fear was even more heighted because social alliances for the purpose of marriage were already difficult to achieve in the camps. Now that village practices were dissolving and sexual mores loosening, Rohingya families were becoming increasingly afraid of attacks on their character and reputation, such as when a daughter is accused of engaging in pre-marital sex or even simply speaking to a non-related man, thereby shaming her family. These moral panics have made camp life challenging and locating a spouse even harder.

In speaking to my interlocutors, it was clear there was a surge in the number of relationships outside of the confines of marriage, particularly amongst the youth. Intimacies were forming in a way that was previously not possible and, furthermore, under a new set of moral expectations. Moral panics and policing were on the rise, and young men and women worked to navigate their way around these new dynamics. When I asked Khushida why this may be the case, she explained:

> In Burma the government was very strict on us and the laws were difficult so now the young people think it is okay to do these things because there is no law. But the thing is, there are more people watching them now than before. Umm ... how should I say this? [*Silence ... she leans in quietly towards me and whispers so that others do not hear*] Now, the situation is even worse. It is so bad now because everybody is in everybody else's business. Men and women are coming together so closely like we never had before. Our villages in Burma were far apart and usually you would only stay with family members. Now different people we never knew are literally living next to you and you see them all the time. Everyone is living so close to each other. Men especially are gossiping about the women and monitoring their every movement.

As described in Chapter 2, since the 1990s, the Myanmar government has required Rohingyas to acquire a permit from the NaSaKa (Myanmar border police force) for marriage, with strict laws prohibiting cohabitation or sexual contact before wedlock, which could lead to 10 years of imprisonment, in addition to already strict religious and moral expectations. Because of the harsh terms of the law, the Rohingyas would view pre-marital affairs not only as 'immoral' but also as illegal and punishable by the state. Khushida notes that while rules on getting married are much easier in the camps, the situation for women in the camps has gotten significantly worse due to the cultural expectations for girls to be shy, polite, and modest and to experience a sense of bodily shame, enforced by heightened regimes of moral surveillance around women's everyday movements and activities as a result of the close living conditions in the camp (Sayigh 2005). I noticed that families and community leaders – particularly *huzur*s and *majhee*s – often complained about the changing nature of unsanctioned relationships. This was especially common amongst unemployed men – both young and old – who could often be found sitting on benches outside makeshift tea shops gossiping about what they considered 'inappropriate' behaviour of young women. In her research, Sayigh (2005: 414) found:

> The reputation of a family, neighbourhood, whole camp, or – later – resistance group would be discussed in terms of the behavior of its *banat* [young unmarried women] … Any scandal involving girls would spread immediately throughout a camp …

This became particularly evident one day when Munni, Zia, and I enjoyed some late afternoon tea in one of the small shacks that sell food in the main bazaar, where the clientele is often a mix of refugees resting in the shade from the afternoon sun and NGO workers stopping for a snack break. A group of men at the table beside us were discussing a meeting that the *majhee* had set up with a number of male elders in the community about 'protecting our women'. Gossip was spreading like wildfire about an 'immoral' woman who was seen speaking to a man that was not her husband, father, or son in a narrow alleyway. When I inquired what the discussion was all about, one man said: 'In Myanmar we did not have such problems. Now our women are exposed to all men. The *majhee* said something must be done about it.' I enquired when the meeting would be held and decided to join them. When the meeting eventually took place a few days later, it was attended by a few *majhee*s, *huzur*s, and other community men. No women were present. One *majhee* spoke at length about how the current arrangements of the camp were markedly different from life in Myanmar – homes in the villages of Myanmar usually had fences around them, and more land was available with villages being spaced out. This afforded Rohingya women much greater freedom within the confines of *purdah* and ensured less mingling with men from outside their immediate family. Further references were made to 'morality' and the importance of being *bhalo mayya-fua* (good girls). When I asked the *majhee* after the meeting about this, I saw how he was quick to suggest that 'Our women must be protected. I urge everyone to know where their daughters are and who they are talking to. Our youth are losing their way. This is the only way we can protect them and maintain the *izzot* of our community.' It was a common notion amongst many of the *majhee*s and elders I spoke to: marriage was the necessary step even for girls as young as 12 to protect them from 'being ruined and destroying the family's reputation', one elder told me. These social risks have become more acute since fleeing Myanmar, as the overcrowded camps and temporary shelters make it very challenging to practice *purdah* properly. Thus, to protect adolescent girls from harassment and assaults, both social and physical, they were often confined to their shelters and married off as soon as possible.

I am reminded of Kathleen Fincham (2010: 44), who in her study of Palestinian refugee women in Lebanon contends that it is 'through narratives of honour and shame and disciplinary regimes of surveillance' that women are policed into compliance in refugee camps. Many of my interlocutors told me that on top of already being worried about safety and food, there was the added pressure of constant eyes and ears on their every move. Young women – whether married or unmarried – noted that they were being monitored with even more scrutiny than before and were held up to certain standards of purity and morality, while men could escape such encounters without being socially sanctioned. And yet, amongst my interlocutors, I found that some young women were still entering into relationships, meeting men in the camps, and falling in love. A few of my interlocutors who were in such 'affairs' reasoned that despite their elders' suggestion that the relations are illegitimate, they insisted that it was only this newfound freedom in the promise of 'marriage for love' that offered a sense of hope as opposed to marriages of convenience, for economic reasons, forced marriage, or otherwise – all of which were taking place in the camp.

Swaleha, in her early twenties, had found love within the camps despite her parents arranging for her to marry a distant relative, Amir Ali. Swaleha's parents had decided on a *manosh'sha biya* (promised marriage) to Amir Ali while they were still living in Myanmar. When the attacks broke out in 2017, Swaleha and her family fled to Bangladesh, losing contact with Amir Ali. For several months there was no news from Amir Ali, and Swaleha moved forward with her life in the camps. She soon began a relationship with a young man, Hasan, who lived with his mother in the shelter next to hers. They attempted to keep it secret, but with news moving fast in the close quarters, their cluster of shelters quickly became aware of the situation. By the time I met Swaleha in April 2018, I learned that it had been two months since she had reacquainted with Amir Ali, who ended up in Nayapara *para* (a settlement at the end of Kutupalong camp) after the exodus. With this new discovery, Swaleha's father was pressuring her to get married and worked to arrange the wedding as soon as possible. Swaleha had already become involved with Hasan and wanted to marry only him. She told me:

> Ever since we found out that Amir Ali is still alive, it has been difficult for me to convince my father that I will marry only Hasan – he told me I am bringing shame on the family. He wants to make me marry Amir Ali but I am going to run away with Hasan if that happens. Women in the camps are just being married at will to different men so for me it is better to be with someone I like. I know there must be a lot of gossip about me. [*She looks down, her headscarf covering her mouth as tears formed in her eyes.*]

Many young women face these tensions within the refugee camps. On the one hand, intimate relations and the concept of relationships and marriage were changing – when once (in Myanmar) it was difficult to have prior relations and meet men, there were more opportunities now because of the close quarters, but also increased surveillance meant that this fear – and moral panic – of the refugee community was in a very literal way *embodied* by these women and affected their gendered identity. Young Rohingya women in many ways navigate within and around these constraints. This is similar to Penny Johnson's (2010: 108) discussion on the way young refugee women in Dheisheh camp in Palestine learned to be aware of the moral judgements and restrictions placed on their bodies and were thus 'agents of change, challenging borders and expanding boundaries'.

'Ideal' Womanhood and Crisis of Femininity

I bumped into Zannat one evening as she was gathering water from the tubewell at the end of her alleyway of shelters and we caught up on some camp gossip. As we walked back to her shelter together, she held the scarf above her head and was looking around suspiciously, making sure not to speak too loudly in case anyone heard her. News about Swaleha's 'affair' had gotten around and she was telling me about it. At one point she said:

Afa, you know there are many girls here who are doing these things with men – we hear all those stories. But that is such a shame for the family. I cannot imagine doing anything like that. Who will marry me then? There is already so many scary stories. I must be patient and then I will get a good *mahr*.

I was fascinated by this discussion with Zannat as it revealed two things. First, she expressed that she did not want to engage in any relationships before marriage because she is 'waiting' for the 'right man' and notes that getting into a relationship just for fun would cause her to not be seen as an 'ideal girl' for marriage. She is aware of the stigma surrounding women's interactions with men and mentions that she is careful not to tarnish her identity as a 'suitable girl for marriage as my family is trying to get me married'. This awareness of the importance of remaining 'suitable' and 'ideal' for marriage is what Greer Litton Fox (1977: 805) notes as embodying the social construct of 'good girl' or 'nice girl' in Muslim communities. These normative value constructs are both a standard for, and goal of, accepted gendered behaviour – a form of social control of women (Fox 1977; Rugh 1984). The second thing that stood out for me was the mention of *mahr*. Zannat insisted that being an ideal wife signified a higher *mahr* payment, which was something she hoped for. *Mahr* was brought up regularly throughout my conversations with my interlocutors, and I was reminded of Karima's wedding (in the introduction of this chapter) when the argument broke out between the bride's and groom's families over the exchange of *mahr* and dowry.

The *mahr* is a mandatory Islamic payment consisting of cash and in-kind items, often including gold and silver, made by the groom to the bride at the *akth* (marriage solemnization ceremony), at which point the payment legally becomes the bride's property. The *mahr* signifies the start of a husband's responsibilities towards his wife (Ripoli et al. 2017). I learned from my interlocutors that during weddings in Myanmar, new brides received gold as a part of the *mahr* – as is common in many Asian Muslim communities. It becomes a form of financial support if a bride is widowed or divorced, and it has become a source of security for many Rohingya women. The value of *mahr* was especially important in the camp context. Some women managed to bring their gold jewellery with them when fleeing Myanmar for Bangladesh, which they then pawn or mortgage for money at the gold stores in the camp bazaar, where shop stalls place blown-up photos of jewellery (instead of the actual gold pieces) on soft, faux-velvet beds of the glass cases. Aid groups only distribute rice, lentils, salt, onions, and a few other basic items to households – any food or clothing beyond these items must be bought or bartered with each other. For that, cash is the main currency for many Rohingyas, and this comes from gold, that is, *mahr*.

Thus, *mahr* has become increasingly crucial for Rohingya women, both Islamically in knowing their worth and value because 'it is our right from Allah', Zannat told me, and in ensuring a form of protection and security should any problems arise within the marriage. The difficulty, however, was that alongside *mahr* the Rohingya community also practices dowry-giving, which is uncommon in other Asian Muslim communities. Even though Islamic religious teachings do not permit the practice of dowry, amongst the Rohingyas, it is common for families of the bride to pay a dowry to the husband's family. As a way to work around official Islamic rulings, the marriage contract in Rohingya custom is preceded by a prenuptial agreement where the dowry is now described as a *hadiat* (gift) (Ripoli et al. 2017). Demands and payment of dowry was a customary practice in Myanmar, and though dowry is illegal in Bangladesh, the Rohingya community still maintains this practice within the camps. I found that amongst the Rohingyas, no marriages are carried out without dowry, as everyone pays some type of dowry, whether in cash or kind. This was the case at Karima's wedding (mentioned at the start of this chapter), when her father insisted that Karima had no *zulm* (rape) done on her and therefore she deserved to get *mahr* – as compared to someone who had been raped, he suggested. I went to visit Karima in her shelter a couple of weeks after her wedding, and her aunt, Tofruda *khala*, was also there. I asked them what really transpired that day at the wedding when the *mahr* discussion took place. Tofruda *khala* explained:

> This is the situation. If a marriage is agreed upon, the guardians just have to inform the *majhee* and he facilitates the *mahr* and dowry. There is no dowry in Islam, only *mahr*. But somehow this dowry practice has become more and more common in our Rohingya culture. In our culture, the more ideal the girl is she will get a good husband and her *mahr* will be higher. Because some of our women had *zulm* happen to them because of the violence, or if they are seen to be bad women talking to lots of men, and not a woman who does *purdah* and follows Qur'an and Hadith, then she is not an ideal woman. These women's *mahr* is lower. They will still get *mahr*, but it will be lower. That's why I don't think it's right to get involved in any kind of bad things because a high *mahr* means an ideal woman. But unfortunately, because Karima was already involved with Hossain before they got married, the fight took place because his family didn't think she was a 'good' match and so they lowered the *mahr* and he only gave her one gold chain.

Karima quickly jumped in at this point, saying:

> Usually we get lots of chains and earrings and bangles! I only got one, isn't that
> unfortunate? But I understand why – I'm okay with it now. Oh, did you see it?
> [*Her face lighting up, moving her scarf away from her chest to show me the thin gold*
> *chain adorning her neck.*] Even if it's not big, I am happy with it.

Tofruda *khala* then continued:

> Listen, *afa*. But the problem we are facing here in the camps is that there are
> not many men. Many of them were killed in the violence in Myanmar or on
> the way here by the army. So, the number of girls here are higher compared to
> the boys. In every house there are many unmarried girls but not enough men.
> So now, the men are not giving *mahr* anymore – instead they are asking for high
> dowry from the families. Women are now becoming worthless – I am sad to see
> that these beautiful young girls are not getting their right given by Allah from
> our men. Allah will punish them for this injustice on *Qiyamat*. As women, our
> worth comes for the *mahr* – it is our individual strength that Allah has blessed
> women with.

This last sentence that Tofruda *khala* stated was particularly revealing as it
hinted at a type of 'crisis of femininity', whereby women are no longer treated
as they were in the past. As the number of suitable and eligible young men
for marriage has decreased, so too has the price of the dowry increased.
Traditionally, the Rohingya marriage process involves a bargain where the
bride's family provides a dowry while the groom's family provides a *mahr*.
The value of the *mahr* varies according to many factors, including the extent
to which the bride is viewed as an 'ideal woman' in society – that is, a young,
virgin girl not having suffered *zulm* nor having had any prior relationships.
However, because of the decrease in the number of men in the community,
the traditional gender expectations correspondingly transformed. Rohingya
women are now being pressured to marry any man who is willing to marry
them, and thus they are having to come to terms with being valued differently as
individuals. Even though the image of an 'ideal woman' persists, a woman who
would traditionally fulfil this image may be unable to gain the corresponding
benefits in the marriage bargain, such as a higher *mahr*.

Rohingya women thus have to come to terms with changes in their gender
identities and the crisis of femininity that arise from the loss of significance
to the notion of the 'ideal woman', which is central to Rohingya femininity.
The lack of eligible grooms has meant that even though fathers and guardians

are desperate to get their daughters and other young women in their families married off, men are asking for exorbitant amounts of money as dowries while giving no *mahr* in return. This explains why Karima's father was desperate to get her married because of the shame of the 'affair' that Karima and Hossain were in. However, Hossain's family was asking for a high dowry, and though Hossain did give Karima a small *mahr* in the end, in most cases, women in the camps do not receive any *mahr* at all, as the practice has become more of an exception than the rule in the camps.

Takoth Sara Mayya-Fua and Lack of Eligible Grooms

Due to the scarcity of eligible grooms and the plethora of available women, men were becoming more demanding in their choice of brides. One young man, Monir, told me that he preferred a younger bride who was a virgin. He remarked:

> The truth is, there are lots of women available now. Many men were killed in Myanmar or went by boat to other countries and left their wives behind, and as you know there were lots of rapes by the army against our women. So unfortunately, there are not lots of men left but we have many women who are unmarried. You will find one house there are three, four, or even five unmarried girls or widows. Now there are many girls that need to get married but not enough men. Because of this we have lots of choice of the kinds of girls we want. The virgins are most preferable as that is looked upon most favourably in our community. Not the girls who are soiled [that is, raped] or widows. [*He pauses for a few seconds then speaks up again.*] Of course, it is not women's fault if that is their situation, but that is our choice.

In the Rohingya community, virgin girls and young women have always been most preferred – this was the 'way we do things in our culture', as mentioned by a *majhee* to me. As discussed in the sections earlier, men preferred to marry 'ideal' girls while also not having any incentive to pay the obligatory *mahr*, which was slowly becoming obsolete due to financial constraints as well as the plethora of choices of young women. The few eligible men now make special demands of the type of women they want and demand higher dowry from girls' families.

The situation is even worse for *takoth sara mayya-fua* – that is, 'vulnerable' women such as rape victims, widows, and discarded or abandoned women. Throughout my time talking to Rohingyas in the camps as well as in discussions with humanitarian aid workers, I regularly came across the term *takoth sara mayya-fua.* This phrase was used to characterize women who were in very difficult situations that would be seen as particularly heartbreaking, even for many Rohingyas who had experienced inexplicable horror in Myanmar. They were often facing a 'double precarity' since they were not only refugees, but in the eyes of society and public consciousness, they were also viewed as 'soiled' women, to quote Monir, limiting their marriage options (Gale 2006; Taha 2019). But in speaking to many of these women, a common thread was the way in which marriage could benefit them – whether through creating kinship ties or accessing camp resources (food, shelter, and so on). Lacey Andrews Gale (2006: 76) found in her research with Fula refugees in Guinea that many women engaged in what she calls 'Bulgur marriages' as a way of 'creating kinship' and marriage ties as a strategy 'to access resources and pursue livelihood activities, actively navigating the opportunities and constraints of their social worlds'.

This is not to say that harmful practices such as forced marriage, early marriage, and marriage-related human trafficking do not take place in the Rohingya refugee camps, especially due to the pressures of maintaining family *izzot*. There were a number of cases in the camps where financial constraints and moral panics have indeed forced families to marry off their daughters without their consent in an effort to remain *izzotdar* (a respectable family), in what Coyle and Jainul (2020) suggest are 'coping strategies'. The pressure to marry young also existed earlier when the Rohingyas lived in Myanmar, and women would recount to me that financial constraints as well as the lack of educational opportunities for women meant that families were eager to have their young girls married off (even while the Burmese government stipulated that marriage below the age of 18 was illegal). This pressure, however, became even more salient in the refugee camps given the limited resources of most families, and some women and girls have become the victims of trafficking to other regions of the world – for example, to Southeast Asia, where a 'demand' for marriageable women exists because of the surplus of Rohingya men.

Nonetheless, beyond these specific harmful practices, in speaking to some of my interlocutors who were seen as *takoth sara mayya-fua*, I found that many women would enter into marriages as a way to 'move forward' with their lives. This was the case of my interlocutor Hasna (introduced in Chapter 2), who lived only with her father, as all the other members of her family were killed in Myanmar. When I visited her in her shelter one evening in October 2019, I soon became aware of a situation that was brewing. Hasna and I sat behind the curtain in the space that was designated for sleeping, next to a small pile of pots and a stove. We were talking for an hour or so when suddenly a group of elderly men stopped by to speak to Hasna's father. In hushed tones, in the space of the room beyond the curtain that separated us, I heard the men inquire about Hasna's experience of being raped in Myanmar. Hasna and I listened as her father recounted the incident to his guests. It was a difficult time for Hasna as she struggled to hold in her emotions, covering her face with her headscarf, though she did not cry. After the men left, her father walked in and we began talking. When the topic of the meeting came up, Hasna sat quietly as her father explained the situation:

> Ever since we have come here, everyone knows about her rape and there is lots of whispering in the community. Many women got *bolazuri zulm* [rape] by the Mog but no man wants to know that it was their wife, daughter, or sister that was raped. I know it is not her fault but what can I do? It is a very big shame for me. I invited the men to the house because I plan to marry her with one of the elderly men who wants a second wife. *Beshi biya* [polygamy] is the only way forward for her. I have decided she will marry next month, *inshaAllah*.

Women who have been raped are having to live with the double-bind of not only living with the trauma of rape but also the 'shame' it brings to the community. I had spoken to Hasna that day and many times after about her thoughts on the arrangement her father had set up for her, and each time the conversations returned to the same point – that she would much rather be married than live a solitary life as she was looking for not just emotional but also social and material support. She remarked at length – in an almost matter-of-fact manner – about why she felt this way, her self-consciousness of her social positioning, and reflections on how to make the best out of her situation:

> We don't have rights in this country. The situation is even worse for girls like me. What can I do? I would rather be married and have someone to take care of me than be all alone. My father is very sick and I cannot take care of him on my own. All women want to be married. Men are the roots of women … we cannot survive without them. Even if he is an old man, he will be my husband. I know that he will help me to support my father and then *inshaAllah* I can have children of my own that will keep me busy. Look at my situation … I have nothing. If you are single and a victim of rape it is more difficult because all the young men want a wife who had no *zulm* done on her. This is usually the main requirement. In this strange country with no work and no family, it is hard to be without a husband. I don't need a lot of things. As long as he is an honest and religious person that is enough. Islam says pious women are for pious men.

If he is good then that is important. Getting married will give me a feeling of peace and give me value in my life again.

I heard many stories like Hasna's. Many of my interlocutors spoke of the difficulties of being a woman who was raped or abandoned by husbands; they were convinced that marriage is the 'appropriate' course of action – even if it meant marrying as a second or third wife. For many of these women, marriage was often the safest and most 'decent' option for preserving dignity and preventing 'social humiliation', as another woman, Sabera, in her late twenties, explained. Sabera was even more forthcoming when she described her decision to accept marriage with an older man who already had two wives. She had arrived in the camps during the mass exodus in 2017 with her two children, aged 8 and 11, along with some neighbours from her village, while her husband had crossed the Andaman Sea to Malaysia one year prior. She explained:

The plan was that he will pay some money to middlemen to help me and my children to reunite with him in Malaysia. We used to talk almost every day the first few months when he got reached Malaysia. Things for him were hard, I know, as he had to spend a few months in jail. The Malaysian authorities were putting all Rohingya refugee men and some women in jail. Then finally he was released and moved to Kuala Lumpur and stayed in a small apartment with 20 other Rohingya men. He used to call me those days – he told me he was making lots of plans and would help me to arrange a middleman to go. Then all of a sudden, I didn't get a call from him for many weeks. I thought maybe things are tough for him so I didn't think anything of it and just prayed to Allah that hopefully he is alive. Then the weeks turned into months and I was getting more and more worried. Eventually it was August 2017 when I came here to the camps. I was still praying for my husband to call me from Malaysia. When I got here, I called another neighbour from my village who had also travelled to Malaysia to inquire about my husband's whereabouts and to inform him that I have made it to Bangladesh safely. The neighbour was not in the same city as my husband so it took him a few weeks to find more information. Later on, the neighbour called me back and told me that he found my husband and that he married someone else. At first, it was devastating for me and I could not bear it. My family members were all killed and I only had one uncle here in the camps that I relied on. Then the proposal came for me from my [current] husband. He is 35 years my senior and has two older wives already. But he is a sincere man and he is taking care of me and my children. This is my only concern … I don't think marriage needs to be only for love – that stage of life is gone for me. I have done this marriage to survive.

Another young woman, 20-year-old Sayeda, had recently gotten married and spoke about the advantage of getting into a marriage in the refugee camp as a way of adapting to the new circumstances. Her family were all killed in Myanmar, and she was staying in the camps with a distant relative from her village. She had accepted an offer for marriage as a way of maximizing on the assistance from humanitarian aid agencies.

> In the camps, NGOs usually give food to couples, and bags per family. When I was staying with my relative there was always struggle for food because we were many people in one shelter and there were not enough bags of rice and *daal* [lentil] for everyone. I had to think about how to improve my situation. I knew that if I marry my husband and I can claim food for our family unit only, that would be better. My parents are not alive. My husband is much older than me but that is okay. He told me he would take care of me like my parents. He bought me everything I need and now there is enough for us to eat without having to ration like I had to when I was staying with my relative. I know my future will be happy because I have my own family.

While entering into marriages to improve a precarious situation as well as reduce insecurity has been well documented in research with refugees in various parts of the world (Hyndman 2007; Kim 2014), marriages involving vulnerable women in refugee settings – like in this case, the *takoth sara mayya-fua* – are often described as a form of exploitation because of the women's precariousness, with such marriages often being quickly associated with forced marriages, child marriages, and so on. However, these stories reveal that rather than simplistic, orientalizing narratives that construe Muslim women – and refugee women specifically – as passive victims fail to give attention to a more complex dynamic at play. These cases show that 'vulnerable' Rohingya women understand the various limitations of their environment and consequently strategize in ways that can provide value to or improve their lives.

However, in all three stories, despite their lives being marked by horrific and traumatic personal events, Hasna, Sabera, and Sayeda all viewed marriage and the creation of 'family' as a 'way to move forward' (Gale 2006). Marriage provided a sense of security, and attaining this security required that they enter into marriages that they may not have otherwise agreed to. This was particularly evident in Hasna's pointed statement: 'Men are the roots of women ... we cannot survive without them.' In the refugee camps, *takoth sara mayya-fua* in particular entered into marriages for protection, support, and companionship since without wider family networks they have fewer resources to keep them afloat. Gale (2006: 78) notes that 'kinship and family, despite chaos and danger, remain central aspects of the human condition and are the life goals around which all else turns'. These cases reveal that despite the many barriers they face, vulnerable Rohingya women are still able to assert agency in the pursuit of their own interests. Saba Mahmood (2001) contends that agency is ultimately the ability to understand one's own interests against traditional expectations – as the stories show, this capacity may be found even in the direst of circumstances.

Thus, Hasna, Sabera, and Sayeda's decisions and desires to marry were shaped by their agency within a context where gender roles and social constructs are established by culture and a society that emphasizes the importance of marriage as a marker of a woman's social inclusion within the community. Such agency is not solely fixated on material interests but rather also seeks to 'attain a certain kind of state of happiness, purity, wisdom, perfection, or immortality', which are brought about by marriage and the social status it entails (Mahmood 2001: 210). In short, these women marry as an agentic act that may at once improve their socio-economic interests and allow them to manoeuvre social structures, while also being a moral and virtuous act that complements widely held understandings of gender and femininity. As Hasna profoundly remarked: '[marriage will] give me value again'.

Conclusion

Marriage and intimate life are an essential part of social continuity and reproduction for refugees, as they recreate the bonds of family that were lost during displacement. Rohingya gendered expectations are being challenged, negotiated, and transformed as young women look hopefully towards marriage as the next step in their lives while simultaneously navigating new freedoms and opportunities afforded to them by camp life. Certain women delay marriage to pursue some of the new opportunities made available by NGOs. Rohingya women also have to manoeuvre the increased intermingling of men and women in the close quarters of the camps. There is a 'crisis of femininity' as the notion of the 'ideal women' is losing meaning given the surplus of men over women, which often meant that women were expected to still maintain a pious image and to pay a large dowry to the groom's family while receiving only a small *mahr* in comparison to the amounts paid in the past. Fathers, brothers, and other household members are anxious to get the young women in their families married, and my interlocutors are coming to terms with how this has affected their gendered identity. *Takoth sara mayya-fua* had a particularly difficult situation in society as they faced the added barrier of being a 'vulnerable' woman amongst the scarcity of eligible grooms. However, using their agency, these women are making strategic choices with regard to marriage as a means of rebuilding their lives.

6

Broken Breadwinners

On Womanhood and Gender Divisions of Labour

Setting Up Shop

I was with Momtaz Khatun inside her small shop one afternoon in June 2018, during the heart of the monsoon season. The summer humidity coupled with the thunderous bellowing of windy rain shook the open thatched dwelling as Momtaz sat at the back, crouched on a small table, intricately embroidering the sides of the dress for her friend's daughter under a lightly dimmed *hariken*, as her husband manned the front table. Eid was only a few days away and Momtaz had two more orders to get through before the holiday arrived. They had set up this small makeshift shop at the end of their lane under a bamboo roof without walls to take orders and sew on demand if anybody required the services. 'There is a lot of demand around Eid time. I know many women are sewing but, in this zone, I am the only one with a shop and so many people know I am here, so they come to me if they need quick service.' Prior to arriving in Bangladesh, Momtaz tells me that she did not 'imagine' ever working for an income, much less having a shop set up for her. In her hometown of Buthidaung, Myanmar, her husband Ahmed was the sole provider, working as a labourer in the village, and her responsibilities revolved primarily around childcare and taking care of the home.

> I am telling you, sister, Allah only knows how we are surviving now. I am trying my best to provide for the family. As you know the men here have no jobs or opportunities and the little money I make from the embroidery is running our household. *Allah'r shokr* [thanks to Allah] I even have this. It's not much, but it's honest work. You know, I used to love embroidering – I always used to do it for fun back in Myanmar, but now it is important work that I need to do to keep my family fed. Especially for my four children. I know it's hard for the men – my husband had a shop in Myanmar and he was self-sufficient to feed our family. But now I am the one with a shop. Isn't that something? Now we are working together. He helps me in the household, and I am helping with getting items. But I do not get a lot of money for my things because my friends

who make orders don't have money so they give me different items. Sometimes
I get money. It depends. But the good thing is my husband and me are working
together. What else can we do? That's the only way to survive.

While the previous chapter focused on the gendered effects of the changing
nature of marriage in the camps, this chapter shines a detailed lens on Rohingya
women's transforming identities and everyday negotiations within the home,
particularly their various livelihood strategies and the new opportunities
brought about through employment, NGO initiatives and trainings, and
other work, which have repositioned both women and men's selfhood in
displacement. Henrietta Moore (1986: 62) succinctly notes that marriage 'links
the formal system of social control and reproduction with the means by which
command over resources and reproduction is achieved'. Thus, marriage is a
site where particular gendered negotiations take place, especially concerning
gender divisions of labour. In many ways, Rohingya women have been forced to
adopt practices and a way of life that are different from their gendered identity,
ultimately affecting their sense of self. The various negotiations of norms and
'expectations' that women engage in are crafted not on a full abandonment of
'culture' or 'the way things used to be' but rather on a careful transformation
of gender identities with new autonomies and encounters. In this chapter,
I explore in depth the bargaining strategies and power asymmetries through
the politics of housework, paid work, and familial/gendered responsibilities
and duties within marriage. The chapter illuminates some of the struggles and
negotiations surrounding transforming gender relations that take place within
a marriage and household. It also captures the changing gender relational
dynamics after displacement and its effects on gender subjectivity, suggesting
that displacement has created not only a crisis of masculinity but also, in some
ways, a crisis of femininity.

Reliance on Humanitarian Aid

Many of my interlocutors, like Momtaz, discussed the changing notions of
gender divisions of labour not only with regard to housework and paid work
in the camps but also in relation to household reliance on humanitarian aid.
The arid conditions of the camps in Bangladesh and the loss of rural ways of
life, including cattle grazing and harvest-ready rice fields, forced Rohingya
refugees to come to terms with changes in traditional livelihood strategies.
I would visit Khatun Khalamma (introduced in Chapter 2) often after being
introduced to her by Momtaz, whose parents knew Khatun Khalamma from

their village back in Buthidaung township. Many refugees, often elderly ones like Khatun Khalamma, often complained about the changes in pre-displacement ways of managing livelihood, as she told me: 'We had animals in Myanmar, now we have nothing. So, the little things we get from the aid agencies we have to sell it for some money or we barter with our neighbours.' As a result of displacement, refugees have become dependent on humanitarian agencies for survival, and in the initial months of their arrival it was common to see large UNHCR trucks stop by the camp a few times a week, with families lining up for a meagre ration of rice, *daal*, and cooking oils.

Khatun Khalamma mentioned to me something that I noticed quite frequently in the camp in the initial days of their arrival – that many refugees would sell part of their food rations as it was 'not enough' to run a household, so much so that it was common that food rations were sometimes sold to other refugees to earn money and purchase more expensive items such as clothes, cooking supplies, and so on. Zannat told me, though hesitantly, that with the relatively large number of members in her household (5 including herself), it was difficult to survive on rice and lentils beyond a few days, and usually other necessary cooking items such as sugar and firewood are hard to come by and not included in the UNHCR rations list. These efforts at gaining cash by bartering items were common amongst families where there was no working member and usually meant that survival depended on a steady flow of food ration handouts and exchanges with other refugees. As such, the usual existence of a rural, agricultural-based lifestyle was now replaced with a more 'economically' driven lifestyle based on cash employment and other 'means of exchange and social identities' (Grabska 2010: 186). This is similar to Gaim Kibreab's (1993) research with refugee communities in Somalia, where the restriction on job opportunities outside of the camp coupled with humanitarian handouts and economic dependency on menial jobs with NGOs resulted in a turn from being a primarily rural-based population to one reliant on selling food rations or the cash economy.

But after the initial months after the mass exodus, the World Food Programme set up a new e-voucher system in early 2018 that was put into place to move away from in-kind distributions and food aid, since the latter involved large numbers of refugees queuing for a long time, often causing 'chaos and confusion', recalled my interlocutor, Aleya. The e-voucher card was set up so that families receive a card loaded with a small amount of money per family member to purchase food at a store set up for five days a week. This new food assistance system was a welcome change for all of the refugees as it provided diversity in types of food and gave families a much wider choice of food options beyond simply rice and *daal*. At the household level, the e-voucher system brought changes in the form of 'patriarchal bargains' particularly around decision-making power over families' resources, as the cards are given to the female heads of households to manage (Kandiyoti 1988). Many Rohingya women shared how issuing individual ration cards allowed them to have a greater role in decision-making and household matters. Tafura, a mother of two, shared something that I heard repeated many times with many other women throughout the camp:

> Before the e-voucher system, usually always the men were responsible for the rations and cards and I was always worried that they will sell it in the market. When my husband was working he used to talk to his friends about what rations we had and they had, and then they would exchange items – important items that I really needed sometimes – and when he would come home I didn't know that he sold it until I asked him. He would just keep the money. Because of his behaviour I would never have what I needed. Then when my husband got sick and couldn't work and walk properly anymore, I took my [2-year-old and 7-year-old] sons with me to collect food and clothes thrown from the relief trucks. We had to run in the mud beside the truck, extremely close to the wheels which was so dangerous. My son was crying to workers 'Give me one! Give me one!' I saw so many people were crushed in the crowd, and my baby almost slipped from my arms and could have been killed that day. There were many people around us who were killed in the stampede during the relief distribution. I didn't know what to do. Then I got so scared after that I again told my husband to go get the rations – he was walking with a stick and I felt bad to make him do it, but what else could I do? I had to feed my family. And then again, I found that he was staying in the market for a long time and negotiating prices with his friends. It was all such a difficult experience. Now that this new system is here I can at least be at peace that I don't have to send my husband to get the rations from the food trucks. I am now responsible for all the food and I have a choice and can make decisions on what I need. My husband does not even bother me anymore about the food and doesn't unnecessarily sell it anymore, which is a big relief.

In her research with refugees in Malawi, Agnes Callamard (1996) similarly found that the ration cards increased women's role and power within a household, particularly with regard to decision-making on household resources and access to food. Women's access to this form of mobility helps sustain the daily needs of their households by themselves without the added pressure of their husbands' overbearing concerns about how to manage the food.

The presence of humanitarian agencies, however, also meant that there was 'greater opportunity', as noted by Momtaz, for participation in the cash economy, not only through taking on small-scale businesses as Momtaz has done but also through the increase in trainings and workshops geared towards 'empowerment', particularly for women. Changes in livelihood strategies had a specific gendered effect on the ways in which Rohingya women now governed their lives within their households and in dealing with a cash-dependent economy. Cynthia Cockburn (1998) reminds us that violence and displacement affect women from the 'bedroom to the battlefield'. Within the huts of Bangladesh's refugee camps, changing gender relations and adjusting to altered gender performances have had a formative effect on Rohingya women like Momtaz. Momtaz's husband, while previously leading the household, is unable to find work and thus Momtaz is the main financial provider. Her example is one of the many I came across while at the camps; whether the women are now sole providers, main providers, or working to supplement the family income – these daily practices within the household impact the gendered relations of Rohingya families. I discuss these negotiations in the sections that follow.

Necessity of Work and 'Acceptable' Roles

Many of my interactions with Rohingyas in the camps were dominated by conversations surrounding the prospect (or lack thereof) of work and livelihoods. Restrictions in the camps meant that there were limited livelihood opportunities available for both men and women, though many Rohingyas felt that the camp provided access to income in a way that was previously not possible in Myanmar. As in many societies, the work carried out by Rohingya men and women is directly influenced by socially constructed notions of 'appropriate' performances of femininity and masculinity. Rohingyas were denied proper employment in Myanmar due to a lack of citizenship status, denial of education, and restrictions on movement. Women were often relegated to spaces within the home largely as caretakers, homemakers, and doing other unpaid work (Farzana 2017). In addition, as they were from a rural background, most of my female interlocutors had limited involvement in a cash-based setting, and they did not have experience in paid employment outside of the home. However, sheer necessity due to conflict caused 'gendered wartime economies' in the refugee context to emerge, though differences among women due to skill level and marital status meant there was a wide range of experiences as a result (Peterson 2008).

I found that while Rohingya women were slowly beginning to work in the camps, most preferred to engage in income-generating activities while remaining *within* their homes because of cultural traditions. Many of my interlocutors shared that in Myanmar, due to the prevailing cultural practices of *purdah*, their daily lives revolved around the home where they were in charge of domestic affairs; conversely, engaging in the public sphere and taking on the role of a breadwinner was viewed as a breach of *purdah*, thus eliciting shame from fellow community members. The refugee camps disrupted this norm by slowly creating opportunities for women to enter the public workforce. Nonetheless, Rohingya women did not immediately jump at this new opportunity; rather, they held a general preference to maintain traditional boundaries of remaining within the home even when they were engaging in income-generating activities. Rohingya women did not seek to abandon the practice of *purdah*, as they viewed it as maintaining their *izzot* and status within their community. Instead, they sought to transform its meaning by incrementally expanding its boundaries in light of the new circumstances in the camp where sheer necessity forced them to play a breadwinning role. These women sought to have their work as breadwinners accommodated within an expanded definition of *purdah*, thereby allowing them to maintain their *izzot*. There are no official jobs for Rohingyas in the camps, as they are not legally allowed to work in Bangladesh – any opportunities that are available in the camps are created by NGOs and humanitarian workers through 'cash-for-work programs' where they earn a modest 300 Bangladeshi *taka* per day (equivalent to about 3.50 USD) (Human Rights Watch 2018). Many of my interlocutors mentioned that even though there were no opportunities in Myanmar, families were nonetheless opposed to the idea of women working for an income. In this new precarious – yet still conservative – setting, traditional Rohingya gender norms govern the work that women now do outside of the house, as they have always largely been limited to homebound activities. The norms of *purdah* continue to determine the scope of women's mobility in the public sphere, thereby governing all aspects of their social and economic life. However, as job opportunities for men remained limited, such gender norms began shifting, showing a slow but steady transformation in traditional mindsets around women's work, thereby granting them greater – though still limited – autonomy outside of the home while allowing them to maintain their *izzot* and remain within the newly perceived boundaries of *purdah*.

I met Tafura (introduced briefly at the beginning of this chapter), a 23-year-old mother of two young boys aged two and seven, when I first arrived for fieldwork at the camp in summer 2017. She had just fled Myanmar several months prior with her children, husband, and ailing elderly mother and had settled into their new life in the camps in a hut amongst a row of huts that housed a few others from her village in Maungdaw, Myanmar. Tafura's father and sister were killed in the Tula Toli massacre. While Tafura's husband initially worked to catch fish, earning a very modest daily income, and got to keep a small share of the catch, his health deteriorated and so she took on work sewing fishing nets. When I sat with her one day in her shelter as she took a break from sewing, her toddler running around with a broken *forfori* (homemade toy airplane), she told me of how she never imagined being in such a position, but she is grateful to be working from home.

> My only responsibility in Burma was to take care of the house and the children and it was the way things were in Burma. But that was because there was no need – my husband was working and providing for the family. As you know in our culture taking care of children and the home is the main priority for women. But I am happy that even though I have to work, at least I am at home and do not have to leave the house for this work. I can still spend time with my children and take care of my family while doing this job. My neighbour's husband takes the fishing nets that I sew and sells them in the market.

Many women, like Tafura, prefer to work within the home and in home-based income-generating activities. Though Rohingya culture often relegates women to the home, this has not stopped them in the camps from creating linkages extending from the shelter to the outside world, thereby working while maintaining traditional understandings of *purdah*. In other instances, the necessity of work has obliged women to leave the household, thus causing women to adopt new norms that deviate from past practices. These subtle negotiations and tensions amongst my interlocutors, which differed according to specific circumstances, evidence the minute, everyday social transformations surrounding the role of women in Rohingya culture. Another interlocutor, Hamida, was running both a sewing business from home and working as a volunteer sewing teacher for an NGO-run sewing co-operative. When I sat with her one day during her break at the co-operative, she spoke of her current situation in the camps:

> I never thought I would get a job in my life. It would have been easier if I could do only my sewing work from my hut instead of having to go outside. Rohingya women, we don't work – and if we do, it's not outside the home. But now it has become a necessity here, so it is better that I also work which is more important

than just being at home. We have lots of different types of responsibilities, and I can now also contribute to my family income which is a good thing. Since everything is different now, we have to think about the future and not stay so rigid in our old ways.

Tafura's and Hamida's (as well as Momtaz's in the introduction) accounts illustrate the changing notions around Rohingya women and work. While previously, paid work – especially outside the home – was frowned upon, there is now a new sense of openness amongst Rohingyas. Previously, families preferred women to stay at home, but as women began to feel an increasing necessity to contribute to household income, many assumed this new role by taking up income-generating jobs, particularly inside their shelters – such as home-based tailoring. However, ever-increasing pressures to make an income have shifted traditional gender roles and performances, with the result that some women have been able to seek work outside the home as well. Zannat has a small tree of green chillis beside her shelter, which she began growing after settling in the camp – she manages to sell a few chillis to her neighbours for a tiny profit. She tells me: 'It doesn't make me a lot of money, but at least I can sell a few for some income for my family since my father will not let me do any work outside the home.' This is similar to what V. Spike Peterson (2009) asserts in her research on war and displacement in Iraq – that 'gendered wartime economies' are affected by conflict and forced displacement by undermining social stability and disrupting traditional livelihoods. Peterson (2008) further discusses what she calls a 'coping economy' emerging out of dire necessity where women become responsible for supporting their families and keeping the household intact as their husbands are out fighting wars, deceased, or unemployed. These changes in the Rohingya camp do not mean the practices of *purdah* have become obsolete. On the contrary, the practice of *purdah* continues to be the widespread norm within the camps. However, its practice has also been circumscribed by the practicalities of earning enough family income to survive. Indeed, these changes in gendered performances can have varying impacts within the household.

Work and Womanhood

Munni (my research assistant) and I waited one afternoon in late April 2018 in Hamida's shelter while she was still at the sewing co-operative where she volunteered. Hamida's husband, Jamil, had welcomed us into the two-room space separated by a flimsy curtain. Hamida's 12-year-old daughter (the eldest) helped her father with the three younger children. The children were all buzzing in and out of the shelter – her second-eldest child had just come home from his religious class in the mosque, while the toddler sat by Jamil. It was evening by the time Hamida walked into the house – her face underneath her *burqa* (full body face veil) covered in sweat from the 2-kilometre walk up the hills in the hot summer sun – as dusk was approaching. She brightly walked in, greeting us with a *salaam* and hugging her children, who ran up to their mother in excitement. She had brought some sweets from her co-operative today and the children rushed off happily, sharing some with the other children in the neighbourhood.

Hamida's weekday mornings were spent completing sewing orders from neighbours and friends. She does the small sewing business out of her shelter – with no sewing machine, she does all the needlework by hand. Much of the sewing she does is through the limited contacts she has through friends and family in neighbouring shelters. She has also taken on volunteering twice a week outside her home as an embroidery teacher – at 11 a.m. she heads out to the co-operative to teach other women needlework, sewing, and sometimes knitting. Though official work opportunities created by the UNHCR in and around the camps are restricted to registered refugees that came in previous waves of migration, the co-operative Hamida works at was set up by a local Bangladeshi NGO that has been keen on setting up opportunities for unregistered Rohingyas after the 2017 mass exodus.

Hamida's days were constantly filled, and though I spent many mornings with her in her shelter, there was little time to actually sit down and discuss topics at length. After she came home that day, Hamida and I sat down in the second room in her shelter, which doubled as a bedroom with a soft, large foam laid out on the floor as a makeshift bed. We just sat down as her toddler ran in holding onto the bottom of her *bazu* and Jamil popped his head into the room to say he would be going out and be back late at night. 'I'm so tired,' Hamida exclaimed, skillfully tending to her toddler and trying to change out of her *burqa* all at the same time. Hamida tells me this was the first time she had worked in her life – she was always skilled at sewing but she never thought to turn it into a business until they fled to the camps eight months earlier. Jamil had been a farmer in Myanmar and was the only breadwinner at home at the time. Since coming to the camps, however, Jamil was unable to find work, and though he briefly had a stint as a brick layer in the camps, paid work opportunities were precarious and oversubscribed. While Hamida took up work sewing, Jamil shifted his time between staying in the shelter with the children and sitting in the market with his friends. When he is out, Hamida's eldest daughter takes care of her younger siblings.

> There are so many times that I wonder if I can manage everything. My days are so busy … there's so much … and you know us women have many things to do. I am happy to do this work. I mean, look at how many children there are – too many mouths to feed. [*She begins whispering and asks her daughter to check if her husband is still in the shelter. She continues once she confirms he has left.*] See I have just come home and he has right away given me all the responsibility of the children. I don't even have time to wash my face. He is at home all day and I am trying to do what I can for the family. Every day I feel less like a woman. Now we women have outside work and also inside work to take care of children – we have to balance everything.

Many of my interlocutors like Hamida struggled to reconcile the new responsibilities and shifting gender roles that come with taking up employment. It was clear that improving the state of women within the community could be tolerated, provided that women continue to perform their traditional gender roles. Changes in traditional male-dominated customs and practices – that is, paid employment – are only positive so long as they remain consistent within a traditional understanding of what is 'acceptable' for women.

'Feeling less like a woman' resonated with many women who were disrupting 'womanhood' – or traditional gendered performances of what it means to be a woman – as working outside the home was perceived as a masculine trait. Although there was a sense of relief and 'happiness', as Hamida notes to being able to contribute to the household, the feeling of being overworked by taking on both 'feminine' and 'masculine' roles is something women are having to navigate. As you walk through the narrow pathways in the camp, some Rohingya women are also taking on new roles that were previously associated solely with men back in Myanmar, including working as brick workers to build roads and other infrastructure run by international NGOs. Ayesha (the woman in her thirties living with her elderly father introduced in Chapter 2) has taken up work as a brick layer. For widows or women with elderly male relatives unable to work, their financial contributions were necessary for family survival, even if it meant the work was something they were not used to before or work that was generally not 'acceptable' for women. After a long day in the sun doing heavy labour, she tells me:

> When I have to struggle constantly outside and then again at home I do all the cooking and cleaning. I don't even feel like a woman anymore. Before providing

was only the man's job but not anymore. I used to be a housewife and had no idea about anything outside of the home. This is the first time I have ever done any kind of work like this – look at me! [*She begins crying.*] I am doing a man's job now – I never thought I will be working out on the road. It is very painful for me. I was a housewife before. Changing from a housewife to a brick layer is very degrading, but I have no other options.

Women like Hamida and Ayesha spoke of the double-burden of doing masculine 'work' and feminine 'caretaking'. And though the women are navigating these shifting gender roles, they are simultaneously having to come to terms with clearly defined gender roles, which can have a strong effect on the gendered identity of what it means to be a 'woman'.

The notion of 'feeling less like a woman' in many ways, as well, brought with it other gendered reconfigurations within the household. There were some cases where my interlocutors felt that taking on jobs and making financial contributions to the family provided new possibilities and skills that permitted greater ability to negotiate decisions within the household, particularly with their husbands, thereby changing notions of womanhood. This is often done by what Deniz Kandiyoti (1988) considers 'patriarchal bargains' where women are able to improve their position for greater autonomy and decision-making. I met Tafura in her shelter one morning while she was completing some sewing tasks. Tafura's husband was heading out to the bazaar and told her he had taken some money, which she kept safe in a small box under the sleeping mattress. They spent a few moments discussing the finances and budgeted the expenses for the week before he left the hut. She turned to me and said:

Did you see how he let me know that he was taking some of the money? When he was the breadwinner most of the time I did not know how much money we had or even where he kept it. Now I am in charge of safekeeping the money. Did you notice that we discuss these things now? I know it's not a lot, but it makes me happy that I have something to contribute and he listens to me. I can make some decisions now.

Just as many women lamented the fact that dire financial need has required them to assume a 'less feminine' role in the household, thereby losing a sense of control over their feelings of womanhood, such work has also granted them greater control over their lives and the lives of their families. As Tafura's case shows, access to an independent income gave some women greater decision-making power within the household and became an important aspect of the 'patriarchal bargain' (Kandiyoti 1988). Ann Whitehead (1995: 39) suggests that the household and family are 'sites[s] of subordination and domination, of sexual hierarchies of many kinds, and of conflicts of interests between its members, especially between husbands and wives'. In this way, some women are able to negotiate their position and power based on their material contribution to the household.

Motherhood and Mobility

A challenge that came up in several conversations with my interlocutors with regard to changing the notions of womanhood was the distractions of working that affected the ability to provide childcare and motherhood. This was a topic that came up in many discussions with many Rohingya women who expressed their worries about not giving enough time to their children, and not being able to care for them, especially the youngest ones. In a conversation with Tafura one evening as we sat outside her shelter, her two-year-old son playing by her foot with a ball of string, she tells me:

> I feel tired, *afa*. I want to be with my children and take care of them how I used to in Myanmar – they are always crying for me, but I feel I can't give them enough attention like I used to. Now they are just running around the camp. In our village in Myanmar we had all our family members and the women used to take care of the children. I am relieved to have the support of this community – my neighbours look after my children when I am not there. But still I get so worried. Sometimes they are on their own – my big one [the 7-year-old] roams around the camps and then comes back in the evening. I don't know even know where he has been the whole day.

While these income-generating activities have given women a sense of ownership over their lives and played a positive role in contributing income for their families, they have not come without challenges, particularly around caretaking and motherhood. Many of my interlocutors expressed worry about how their preoccupation with their jobs and having to navigate various responsibilities both within and outside the household have been affecting their relationship with their children. Hamida tells me her eldest daughter – the 12-year-old – has started to feel resentment towards her, and she is often plagued with the difficult expectations of being a 'good' mother while also providing for the family. She explained:

> One day my daughter told me I was working too much and not there to help her at home. She said she was happier in Burma because I was at home with

her and we used to spend time together and play. But now I don't do any of that anymore. I fled Burma to save their lives, but now I can't even be part of their lives. I am always so busy and tired. I'm trying to manage everything ... [*She trails off.*]

Hamida's narrative is a poignant reminder of the difficulty in grappling with the various emotions and multiple responsibilities of displacement, particularly as extended family networks, from which women normally draw much of their strength and support, have been transformed or lost. Whereas in Myanmar there was a large network of family and relatives who could be relied upon for help, the loss of these networks meant that with shifting responsibilities of employment and motherhood within the refugee camps in Bangladesh, Rohingya women were having to navigate the emotional and physical tensions surrounding worth and value – particularly of being a 'good' mother. Women were now having to rely on their (sometimes unemployed) husbands to manage childcare while they were at work, thereby transforming the traditional division of responsibilities within the marriage and gender division of labour in Rohingya culture. This was particularly evident in Hamida's case, whose husband Jamil bears co-responsibility for their children. While that may be true in Hamida's case, for some of my other interlocutors, in the absence of husbands and fathers of their children, they are now having to navigate a new set of challenges associated with working in the camps and the heavy demands of both household labour and work. As Sayigh (2002: 323) reflected in her own research with Palestinian refugees:

> Marriage controls women beforehand through the importance attached to virginity [as we saw in the previous chapter] and afterwards through the responsibilities of childbearing and housework, and the many kinds of social labor attached to the housewife role.

Many of my interlocutors were raising families of several children while also engaging in some type of work for wages or voluntary work. There were added anxieties of raising children in the camps during this period of uncertainty and hardship, particularly the worry of being left alone or the shifting responsibilities from parents to their children to take on household tasks.

Women's views of gender divisions of labour are not homogeneous, of course, but depend on the individual personal histories and how each individual presents his or her gendered self in relation to collective situations and discourses (Moore 1994). In some cases, there was also dissatisfaction with their increased mobility. In line with their 'feeling less like women' and having to negotiate their womanhood as outlined in the previous section, one of the interesting discussions I heard was about women's experiences of mobility. Many of my interlocutors expressed dissatisfaction with their increased mobility, citing that the material benefits are much less than the social costs they incur. A few said that the livelihood crisis, and the necessity of spending more time outside the home, have opened up opportunities for them. But they also asserted that this increased mobility would not be possible or of value if it did not result in material benefits to sustain their households. In many of our conversations, some of my interlocutors expressed a desire to return to their traditional life – that is, a life where they stay at home and men work to provide for the household. It was indeed a life that they knew, understood, and yearned for. New access to work and greater mobility were not something to aspire towards but rather something to be cautiously taken up if necessitated by circumstances. A great deal of my interlocutors did not necessarily see increased mobility and 'work' as a free choice – especially middle-aged women with childcare responsibilities – but rather something that had to be done out of necessity, and its effects on the household had to be negotiated carefully.

Crisis of Masculinity and 'Good Wives'

Alongside these various gendered performances, changing gender identities as a result of conflict and forced migration for both men and women can often result in gender-based violence. In a discussion with a *majhee* and a group of Rohingya refugee men, the *majhee* mentioned to me that the initial reliance on the UNHCR was a welcome relief for men who had also suffered tremendously during displacement. One of the men in the discussion group, Kader Imam, an elderly *huzur* of one of the makeshift mosques in the camp, noted:

> We were grateful to have food and water and safety. The UNHCR food rations was very helpful and we did not have to bear the trouble for providing for our families since we had nothing. In Burma we were the breadwinners, but now we have no money, no job, nothing. We ran away from Burma only with our clothes. The help from UNCHR took away responsibility for providing for our families because we had no means. But now they have limited their rations to only a few items and it is not sufficient. We have to now provide again but there is no work for us. It has been very difficult.

The initial arrival into the camp meant that the role of the UNHCR and the international community in providing food rations as well as shelter, education, and medical attention took away the 'breadwinner' role of men. The humanitarian relief allowed Rohingya men to navigate the gendered expectations of being the 'provider' of the family. Over time, however, as rations waned and men were required to make up the difference with other sources of income, men grew increasingly frustrated, dejected, and emasculated due to an increasing sense of purposelessness as they were largely confined to idling around their shelters or at tea shacks in the bazaar (Gardner and El-Bushra 2016; Ritchie 2018). Without any form of livelihood opportunity or work life outside the household, refugee men are no longer able to serve as the breadwinners and protectors of their families, which undermines their sense of 'manhood' within the 'gendered relationship', leaving them less confident and ashamed of their state (Gardner and El-Bushra 2016; Ritchie 2018). In a similar case, Nadia Elrashidi (2005: 10) writes on her research with Palestinian refugees that 'the crisis of the male breadwinner is a gendered crisis ... this places enormous stress on gender roles'. Several other scholars have also detailed experiences of refugee men's gender identities being undermined, particularly their masculinity and gendered 'expected' roles as providers, protectors, and decision-makers (Turner 1999, 2000; Brun 2000). As traditional notions of masculinity and femininity related to 'appropriate' gender roles and relations in certain cultural contexts transform or shift in exile, in some cases I learned of various instances of Rohingya women in the camps experiencing an increase in domestic violence. Some of my interlocutors told me that they continue to endure rape and abuse within their marriages out of fear of being alone with their children with nowhere to go.

In a quiet moment one day, as we walked back together to her shelter from the co-operative where she volunteered, Hamida confided in me some news. She told me:

Jamil sometimes cannot tolerate that I am providing for the family and he is not. He gets very angry and sometimes beats me. It is getting tougher day by day. The worst thing is that whatever little money I am getting, I don't want to give it to him because I know sometimes he wastes the money to buy *yaba* [drugs] from the market. But I am trying my best to hide some money and I tell him that I have not yet been paid. Even if it's very little, I usually hide the money in my pots and pans because I need to think about my children and save it for them. I know he will never go near the pots. But I also know he is violent because he doesn't have a job – I understand his position. We have so little here and there is not so many opportunities for men, so I can understand his frustrations and why he is angry.

Hamida's account reveals the way in which she must navigate her circumstance – hiding the money from her husband in the cooking pots because she knows Jamil will not go near them. Her mention of this particular tactic reveals a particular feature of Rohingya culture where the power of men over women is circumscribed by the complementarity of their roles in the household – a man cannot interfere in the 'feminine sphere' (that is, i.e. in the kitchen which is full of pots) as that would go against the cultural expectations and prescribed roles of men and women. However, the fact that women were at the same time now entering into paid labour (that is, the 'masculine sphere') resulted in men also having to navigate their masculinity as they perceived a threat to their manhood without an ability to assume control of their circumstances.

Hamida confessed to me that her constant navigations and negotiations about having to deal with the violence inflicted by her husband have deteriorated her own well-being and created further tensions within her household. Men's frustrations are elevated because of the gendered norms within Rohingya culture – men should be breadwinners while women should look after the house (Akhter and Kusakabe 2014; Women's League of Burma 2002). The change in traditional family roles and responsibilities aggravates and frustrates men, causing increased tensions within the family (Burnett and Michael 2001; El-Bushra 2004). When I spoke to Hamida's husband, Jamil, he complained of not being able to provide for his family in a traditional role, which strained relations with his wife and increased problems at home, sometimes leading to violence.

> I feel angry and ashamed as a man that I don't have a job and am not able to provide for my family. I do all the work in the house because Hamida is not home in the daytime. I know she is now the breadwinner and I am not, but I am still a man. I am the husband, so I have the authority in the house. As a wife she should always obey me. But this is the problem – she never wants to listen to me anymore.

As family dynamics begin to change, as in Hamida's case, erosion of male power and privilege at the socio-economic level such as through loss of economic opportunities, unemployment, and their inability to 'reconstruct' their position within the boundaries of the family can have consequences resulting in gender-specific violence (Huseby-Darvas 1994; Colson 2003).

When I sat for tea with a group of men one day in the market with my research assistant Zia, it was clear there was a significant amount of frustration amongst Rohingya men around losing control of their family, idleness, and the social pressure of carrying out 'masculine responsibilities'. A 22-year-old unmarried man, Ashfaq, living with his mother and two younger sisters complained about the added responsibilities of taking care of the family and the difficulties of finding employment. With hints of tears in his eyes, he spoke to me while staring blankly at the wall:

> I tried so many things – I tried to get work in the camps and even sometimes went outside illegally without the army seeing me but then my friend got caught and went to jail so I stopped trying. I am angry about everything. What is there for us to do? We sit all day – either here or in our shelter. In our culture if the man is providing for the family there is respect from the community. All of us here are trying our best – nobody can say that we don't – but we are not getting enough opportunities. It is hard to stay at home like women.

These frustrations expressed by Ashfaq were reminiscent of many unemployed men that I spoke to. The sense of powerlessness amongst Rohingya men was prevalent throughout the camp. It is a common sight to see large groups of men sitting by the side of the road throughout the day, sometimes talking to others, mostly looking out at those passing by. The lack of opportunities for men within the camps and the growing sense of helplessness had serious effects on their self-perception.

This was especially evident in the way marital violence was used, as highlighted by Hamida's narrative earlier – particularly wife-beating. Family affairs within the home are a site of control and gender power, and wife-beating is thus an expression of this power. Hamida mentioning that her husband Jamil would 'beat' her because he could not provide for the family – this was a fairly common statement amongst my married interlocutors, especially when it concerned the economics of the household. The inability to act as the breadwinner of the family and the loss of control in certain circumstances lead to feelings of powerlessness and frustration amongst men. The household remains one of the few venues where men are able to retain control of their circumstances, and violence is a means through which men release their frustration on those over whom they have control.

Karima, the newlywed wife introduced in Chapter 4, had mentioned to me a few weeks after her wedding that Hossain had become violent when she expressed interest in attending some workshops geared towards Rohingya women run by an NGO. Henrietta Moore (1994) discusses the notion of 'thwarting' when thinking about threatened gender identities. She suggests that '[thwarting] can be understood as the inability to sustain or properly take up a gendered subject position, resulting in a crisis, real or imagined, of self-representation and/or social evaluation' (151). When I later spoke to Hossain about his thoughts on the gender programming in the camp, he told me:

> Let me tell you, *Afa*, if my wife will be out of line, I will beat her right away. I have no shame in it. Our culture does not allow women acting in strange ways. And I know sometimes the foreign NGO men teach strange things to our women. It will not be appropriate for my family status. Men must always be in charge of the family. I have made the decision that Karima cannot attend.

Hossain's discussion of culture is closely linked to 'honour', or *izzot*, for the Rohingyas, and any deviations from a perceived sense of 'appropriate' behaviour warrants violence and wife-beating. It looks at the increasing resentment by Rohingya men towards NGOs because of the opportunities provided to women.

Due to the changed familial dynamics brought about by the dispersal of extended families throughout the camp, Rohingya women now have to contend with these changes, particularly in resolving marital disputes. Traditionally, when problems occurred within a marital household, a wife could get help from her husband's relatives, or even possibly return to her father's home if her husband was being abusive, or rely on her brothers' and other male relatives' support. A woman's brother would usually be available to provide support in case of severe abuse by the husband or his family. One time, Shofika had told me on speaking about her brother Kobir:

> Brothers in our culture are very important. That is why when I knew Kobir was alive I had to be with him. Even after a girl is married the brother is always there to help you if you need anything. We respect our brothers a lot in our culture – like a father figure – he is always there to protect me.

Unfortunately, for many of my interlocutors, these strategies became unavailable as only a small number of families arrived at the camps as a whole unit after the violence in Myanmar (as Chapter 3 discusses in depth). Thus, with now fragmented and broken families, many women had no one who could aid them against their husbands' violent behaviour, or whom they could call upon for assistance, such as the extended family. As it was impossible to reconstruct traditional village settings, this change in settlement patterns affected many of my interlocutors' ability to get recourse in case of violence and spousal conflict. Many of my interlocutors thus faced not only physical isolation from thick and rich family networks but also death, with the absence of mechanisms that could socially discipline certain acts of violence in the family when men acted from the position of physical strength (the next chapter looks at the greater reliance on the community *majhee* for support and its implications).

Similar to Hamida's situation, another woman, 26-year-old Kulsum who had five children, told me that after she and her family were displaced from Myanmar and her husband was unable to find work, she has had to support the family while also enduring his violent behaviour. In Myanmar, her husband had been a fisherman and he relied on their small plot of land to provide for his family. His breadwinner status was a central feature of his masculinity and how he wished to be perceived in society – that of the primary, respected leader of the household. It was through this role as the breadwinner of his family that he maintained his status with the wider community. Kulsum thus told me, similarly to Hamida, that she 'understands' why her husband resorts to violence:

> I didn't experience this type of violence before in Burma – he used to be slap me a few times but ever since coming here it's a different type of violence. I can't explain it. There is a lot of built-up rage inside him and he will just randomly hit me for no reason. Sometimes I wonder why he is behaving this way because he knows we are all struggling. Everybody is suffering so it is not only him. I try to explain to him but he still beats me. I get scared but then I have to think of my five children. At least we are still one full family. There are so many families here that don't have a mother or a father – so I will tolerate it from him. Also, if I don't tolerate this behaviour, what will people say? I know society will say I am a bad wife and do not know how to respect and obey my husband, so it's better to bear this than have so much gossip about me.

For Hamida and Kulsum and many Rohingya women like them, violence was something to be tolerated to be able to support children and maintain some sense of household stability – especially in their precarious situation. Except for a few exceptions, almost all the women who suffered violence from husbands did suggest that violent behaviour from their husbands took place even before arriving at the refugee camps. However, my interlocutors still minimized the violence that took place in Myanmar, rather suggesting that being in the camps and the wider economic issues in this new situation caused men to be jobless and restless, and they attributed their husband's violent behaviour to these specific harsh circumstances. Such remarks should not be interpreted as meaning such violence was uncommon in Myanmar, but rather that Rohingya women intentionally downplayed past incidents of violence directed at them from their husbands as a means of understanding this violence within a wider set of events brought about by forced migration that radically disrupted the previous balance in gender roles – as Hamida says, she 'understands' why her husband is frustrated. Unemployment amongst men fueled their aggression, and by bearing their husbands' violence, women were 'sharing' their husbands' frustrations while also maintaining the cohesion of their whole family.

While male aggression may be associated with male domination and authority, it may also point to male fragility. Within the context of the Rohingya camp, male violence is a sign that 'the perpetrator of violence is threatened and experiences thwarting' (Muhanna 2016: 107; Moore 1994). Men find themselves in deeply unsettling circumstances as they no longer serve as the primary breadwinner of the family, which was an important source of their masculine identity. By enduring violence, women maintain their own images of masculinity even while other aspects of masculine identity come under threat – such as still viewing their husband as the sole authority in the house. Furthermore, as Kulsum explained, Rohingya society would accuse her of being a 'bad wife' unable to fulfil her duties by standing by her husband at a time when everyone is facing joblessness. Many Rohingya women sought to present their husband as facing difficulties but still maintaining their masculine qualities – such as being the head of the household – a narrative that allowed them to position themselves as a 'good wife.'

One interlocutor, 24-year-old Rasheda – whom I met through Tafura as they both sew fishing nets – whose husband has been unsuccessful in finding a job, emphasized how an 'ideal wife' does not destabilize the 'normal' gender order in a household at a time when her husband is facing difficulties but rather should support him. She told me:

> He doesn't have a job, but what's the problem? He is still the man of the house, no? Even though I am bringing in the money, all final decisions are taken by him. Sometimes he consults me, sometimes he doesn't. Our culture is not about man versus women – everyone has the appropriate position that Allah has given us. A man is a man and a woman is a woman. We cannot reduce his value because he no longer has a job.

Through Rasheda's narrative, we see how women are able to construct a compelling narrative of being a 'good wife' by upholding their husband's dignity. In a Rohingya household, a woman's status is linked to reliance on her husband and his masculine authority. Women who suffer aggression and violence from men may also seek to show respect to those same men as doing so not only maintains the gendered order within the household but also preserves the woman's positive image of their husbands. Rohingya women thus perpetuate a familiar idealized image of masculinity despite the gender instability that emerges within the household due to a jobless husband having a wife who works.

In speaking with my interlocutors, I found that women did not want to be seen as dominating their husbands since their own self-respect as 'good wives' would be undermined by having their husbands suffer such shame. Even if they suffered violence, Rohingya women expressed their preference for a masculine and assertive husband in their household. Any perceived sense of domination by the wife brought about by her contribution to the finances of the household were explained to me in a way that left the husband as the ultimate authority.

Moore's (2007) concept of a 'fantasy' helps us make sense of the behaviour of these women. Fantasies represent identifying with certain social values and ideology but not necessarily with individuals' wishes. Rohingya women play out a dual fantasy of wanting to represent their husbands as 'masculine' figures while at the same time wanting to maintain a level of control over their own affairs. By presenting men and women in certain ways and as fulfilling certain roles, a relatively stable gendered order may be maintained, even if this outward representation masks underlying tensions and crises concerning gendered identities. The representation of this gendered order can help provide stability within a given environment. It is as one middle-aged man, Rafiq, once told me:

> You cannot imagine, *afa*, the way men have no jobs and no opportunities, it is something unbearable. But even though my wife is making money and bearing the burden, she does not let me feel inferior. She knows that it is not because of lack of manliness that men cannot find jobs, but it is the situation we are in that is out of our control. International humanitarian aid has made us into beggars.

Thus, as these stories show us, Rohingya notions of masculinity and femininity have not been radically or even substantially transformed by a new gender division of labour in the camps. Instead, men and women continue to be represented through narratives supporting 'ideal' notions of masculinity and femininity, thereby sustaining narratives of idealized gender roles even when these roles are shifting in reality.

Conclusion

Displacement has repositioned both men's and women's selfhood, especially as it relates to gender expectations surrounding labour within and outside of the household. The loss of men's employment has forced women to take up paid work, which was never an option in Myanmar. While some women have welcomed these opportunities as a means of improving their negotiating and decision-making power within their marriage, others struggle to reconcile their new responsibilities and shifting gender roles, causing a crisis of femininity and a questioning of their sense of self.

Men were largely unable to find work and fulfil their roles as breadwinners in the household. As a result of men's reduced power and privilege within the home, women faced increasing violence, especially in relation to their paid work. Despite such violence, many Rohingya women continue to subscribe and adhere to expected gender 'ideals' of masculinity and femininity in order to avoid destabilizing the household. For Rohingya women, this means forbearing violence from their husbands as their ability to uphold the 'masculine' image of their husbands – particularly given the difficulties men face in fulfilling their traditional role as breadwinners – also reflect on their own 'feminine' ability to be 'good wives'.

7

The Price of Development
On NGOs and Gender Programming

'It Is a Different World'

Through the narrow, dusty pathways of the camps, various NGO initiatives in the form of training centres and women-friendly spaces have emerged to teach women, according to one NGO worker, 'vocational pathways to sustainable livelihoods', by providing knowledge on topics such as self-empowerment, confidence-building, and gender equality. Many of my interlocutors alluded to the fact that the presence of humanitarian aid organizations provided opportunities that they were not afforded before in Myanmar, such as special assistance and training on domestic abuse and other forms of gender-based violence, for example. These had a profound effect on the way gender relations and roles were changing in the camps, particularly the way gender divisions of labour and ideas were reshaped. Khatun Khalamma found that the presence of a large number of humanitarian agencies and increased NGO initiatives introduced Rohingyas to 'things we are not used to'. She tells me:

> All these NGOs have brought so many things we did not know before. My neighbours are attending classes and workshops. It is so different from how we used to do things and now look at the women – they are more active than we ever used to be. It is a different world than what we know.

The UN Inter-Agency Response Team, in cooperation with the Bangladeshi government, led the coordination of the humanitarian response, including other development initiatives and programming. Strolling through the camps in the mornings among the bustle of activity in the markets, one can see men gathered around tables in makeshift teahouses watching news on television sets and women indoors tending to the housework. One notices Rohingyas, young and old, holding mobile phone sets and watching the news and connecting to loved ones across borders and oceans. (Note that a mobile phone blackout by the Bangladeshi government took place starting in the fall of 2019 – when

I conducted my fieldwork in 2017–2018, they were still readily available and in use.) The arrival of NGOs brought access to technology, television sets in the bazaars, and the presence of the international community through NGO workers, fieldworkers, researchers, and other regular foreign involvement. As Momtaz explained to me:

> In Myanmar we were shut out from everything and lived in despair. Even though life is not easy here [in Bangladesh] we have more access to the world and different types of ideas and people. We are learning many new things.

These varying exposures to flows of people and information within the camp provide more 'access', as Momtaz notes, to the outside world via such technologies as television and phone. It is a type of development that Khatun Khalamma suggests is 'different' from the rural life that Rohingyas are familiar with.

In this chapter, I analyse how the wave of humanitarian aid agencies that have spread across the camps has also played a role in altering the gender dynamics of the camp. Rohingya women regularly interacted with aid agencies and NGOs, something that did not take place in Myanmar. The hundreds of NGO offices all working to assist the 'largest refugee crisis in the world' have shifted the way many Rohingya women understand the ways in which they can effect changes in their lives in ways that were previously not possible. This 'gender micropolitics of NGO assistance', as Szczepaniková (2008) suggests, requires careful evaluation to understand the ways in which development efforts influence Rohingya gender dynamics in the camps. The chapter thus discusses women's exposure to, and contact with, the NGO industry and gender programming and how this directly impacts and transforms gender asymmetries.

'Feminizing' Refugees

Within a few weeks of refugees arriving in Bangladesh, I noticed a large number of aid organizations and NGOs suddenly becoming active in the camps, with a strong focus on implementing gender equality strategies, and other awareness-raising, empowerment, and assistance programming. Organizations focusing on humanitarian assistance within the camps vary in size, from large international aid agencies such as the UNHCR, UNICEF, Save the Children, and Médicines Sans Frontières with hundreds of staff members, among others, to local organizations with only a handful of staff and limited resources. The camp also hosts civil society organizations such as BRAC that provide skills training and help to foster social enterprises in the camps. Organizations operating on faith-based principles, such as Islamic Relief, also occupy the humanitarian landscape. As the presence of aid agencies and NGOs increased in the camps, so too did the implementation of gender workshops and trainings on human rights and gender issues. It is not uncommon for an NGO-run women-friendly space to be filled with posters on the wall – one in particular, I noticed, was drawn by a Rohingya woman picturing a man and woman holding hands, and in big bold letters in the Rohingya language written below was 'men and women must work together'. The women-friendly space staff member spoke at length about the 'importance' of this message:

> This is the message we want women to know – that they are important members of society. And we want them to know that when they are educated, their whole family will be educated and in turn the whole society will be educated.

These gender messages through posters and signage in front of NGO buildings were prevalent throughout much of the camp alongside the implementation of gender equality workshops targeting women's empowerment and 'including men in the process', as another NGO worker told me. Over time, it was clear that much of the programming implemented by NGOs were primarily geared towards women and/or the safety of women. These included preventing gender-violence workshops, hygiene and sanitary workshops, training courses for sewing and handicrafts, dealing with mental health programming, and women's safety in the camps. With almost 60 per cent of Rohingyas in the refugee camps being women and girls, one NGO staff member mentioned to me – just prior to leading a workshop focused on women's safety, preventing violence against women, and women's empowerment:

> Our priority right now is the safety of women. We want to engage the whole community so we have included both men and women in this workshop in protecting the safety and needs of women and girls. Our main goal right now is to ensure that women are empowered and so men learn about women's rights and gender equality that will help them lead proper and meaningful lives in the camp.

The workshop, run by a local NGO, took place in an open shelter that was empty save for a few large mats laid on the ground. The shelter was often used as a meeting space for staff members as well as for other meetings and workshops. When the room filled up with about 30 people, including 12 men, women were encouraged to sit on the mat in the front of the hall while men were seated at the back. I noticed there was an active attempt to get the women to participate in the discussions, particularly when discussing the importance of gendered protection with regard to preventing sexual and gender violence, such as rape and domestic exploitation. Men were asked to participate only towards the end if they had any questions about the material. The workshop revealed a few interesting points. Firstly, a focus on 'empowerment' and equality between the sexes was perhaps not necessarily directly intended to shift gendered behaviour, but nonetheless, workshops such as the ones I attended discussed topics that sometimes directly contradicted what was generally acceptable in Rohingya culture. Second, this focus on 'prioritizing' women was not well received by many Rohingya men. One of the male participants in the workshop later told me:

> It is good that they are including us in the discussions of women's rights and safety, but why are there no job trainings for us men? We are shut out from all the workshops and the UN is always focusing on them and giving more opportunities for them. But we are sitting here jobless.

In this way, the overwhelming presence of NGOs, UN, or humanitarian agencies results in what Szczepaniková (2008) notes as the 'feminisation of the refugee clientele', where women are often regarded as the 'ideal' refugee 'client' by NGOs – more 'ready' to comply with new gendered ideals. Women are viewed as being more susceptible to various forms of abuse or exploitation within the camp – a view with a real element of truth – and thus trainings through workshops and information dissemination is a means of addressing this problem. In this way, NGOs could claim to be providing a corrective to the gender-based challenges arising in the camps by disrupting prevailing gender dynamics. Men, on the other hand, are seen as 'potential problem-makers', for example, because of the violence they may inflict on their families. NGOs are less inclined to make men-specific programming because of their supposed disinterest in participating in the workshops. The participation of men in these workshops was arguably instrumental, as NGOs could claim to be sensitizing these men to notions of women's empowerment. The advocacy by NGOs of a discourse of 'empowerment' sought to provide Rohingya women with concepts that could help them negotiate new gender roles and potentially forge a new gender identity within the camps. However, these NGOs did significantly less to incorporate men into their efforts, thus highlighting the one-sidedness of their efforts and calling into question their ability to be fully effective tools for transformation.

'Transforming' Rohingya Womanhood

When displaced to the refugee camps, Rohingya women lost a number of community mechanisms, such as the support of extended family that provided them a level of safety within the domestic sphere; nonetheless, displacement also made new safety mechanisms more readily available. Some Rohingya women were now taking advantage of this refugee 'feminization' and using it to negotiate greater opportunities for themselves. I noticed that one large international organization, for example, had posted information – ranging from women's safety to health and hygiene tips, as well as information on upcoming workshops – on a board outside their makeshift office and women-friendly space in the camps. But the reality was that the vast majority of the targeted recipients – Rohingya women – either were illiterate and/or had no access to the board because of restrictions on their movement, whether or not by choice. A staff member of the NGO told me that these workshops were intended to 'empower' female participants with various skills and knowledge. And indeed, a few Rohingya women were keen on using NGO workshops and the education and skills they were gaining as a way of crafting greater freedoms and rights for themselves.

One afternoon, after a workshop finished, I walked back with Khushida to her shelter. As the remaining child of her parents, Khushida's father Ahmed allowed her to explore her interests, despite his hesitation. While growing up in Myanmar, Ahmed had taught Khushida and her siblings how to read Burmese, and she is one of the very few literate Rohingya women in the camps. There were limited educational opportunities in the camps – only a few NGO-run schools for young children. The only access to skills for women, young and old, was by way of workshops, which Khushida was actively engaged in. With her language skills, she was considered a role model and often participated heavily during workshops – this allowed her to take up a position at a children-friendly space teaching Burmese to Rohingya children one day every two weeks. She told me:

> There are not many Rohingya women that can read and write and certainly not here in the camps. We did not have any opportunities in Burma but we have them now and that is very important. Many of these training programs

are helping women like me learn about our rights. I learn so much from these workshops. I am grateful to have this small job so I can help my parents. I know they're just waiting for me to get married … [*she pauses to laugh out loud*] … but at least for now they let me participate in these activities, when it is not possible for many women to do so.

Khushida's account illustrates the growing sense of excitement with the opportunities available to Rohingyas in the camps, which has allowed her to negotiate a position within her household through the material contribution she brings by way of income. She notes the way NGOs have targeted women and are keen to 'empower' them in an effort to make a difference in their families and communities. UN and NGO staff were often keen to highlight stories like Khushida's as 'success stories', bringing her to meetings and encouraging her to speak up on behalf of Rohingya women. Girls like Khushida – though there were not many in the camps – often used the language of rights and empowerment taught in these workshops to negotiate their freedom within the limited space of the camp (Ortner 1996). In this way, the correct discourse helped further consolidate the authority of these women, who were not only viewed as literate but, moreover, as bearers of rights because of their literacy. I met other young women like Khushida who had attended NGO workshops and were subsequently employed by these same NGOs to visit homes throughout the camps to encourage others to join workshops – especially adult women – essentially going door to door informing them of the benefits of such workshops.

For women like Khushida, the presence of NGOs brought with it a new consciousness. As Sarah J. Mahler and Patricia R. Pessar (2010) suggest, movement across geographic scales and social locations is not crisply defined in the way one physically moves across a border. Gendered identities and relations are negotiated across locations and geographic borders. As such, Khushida's gendered identity was not relinquished once she was displaced from Myanmar, and neither was it stuck in time. Instead, she had to negotiate and recreate her identity and gendered practices, which were transformed not just by her current situation in the camps but also by her altered aspirations about the future. She frequented NGO workshops, became acquainted with women from other countries who either worked at the NGOs or visited the camps, and observed other behaviours and roles by NGO staff that were different from Rohingya norms as she traditionally understood them. Through these experiences, Khushida realized that gendered practices and concepts of 'womanhood' existed that were different from Rohingya norms, and how they play out affects visions about the future for Rohingya women. For Khushida, this ultimately fostered a new way of understanding Rohingya 'womanhood', where women not only learned of their rights but also became the bearers of those rights amongst fellow Rohingya women in the camps.

Competing Ideologies

While providing some positive opportunities for Rohingya women, NGO workshops were not without criticism, and there were differing views on womanhood and the role of humanitarian organizations in intruding on cultural and customary norms. This language of NGO rights and the hallmarks of a new type of womanhood – that is, being outspoken, participating in workshops, and being active in public spaces – were frowned upon by many Rohingya men and women in the camps. This push for women's empowerment was consistent across lay and faith-based NGOs. While Islamic, faith-based NGOs have religious motives for their humanitarian assistance, the delivery of that assistance took the form of workshops that pushed for women's rights and greater participation in the public sphere. Khushida's father Ahmed woefully told me that he was worried about the way NGOs were pushing for 'rights' in a way that provided newfound freedoms that many feared were against the *izzot* of women in Rohingya culture, indicating that the gender programming was challenging their masculinity and gender identity:

> I have allowed Khushida to go out and participate in the NGO activities, but there has been a lot of comments from my neighbours about my daughter because she is unmarried and they say she is getting influenced by these Western ideas. They say that she is spreading ideas about women's rights and many other things our culture is not familiar with. They say that I have already lost two children and now I am slowly losing my last one to the West. People in our society say many terrible things. I worry about her safety, but I also want her to do something with her life. We did not have any opportunities in Burma – here she can do something, *inshaAllah*.

Kandiyoti (1988: 286) suggests that 'it is only at the point of breakdown that every order reveals its systematic contradictions' – which, for the most part, took place for Rohingyas after displacement. Certain gender and social relations were contested, renegotiated, and transformed, as in the case of Khushida and her father's approval of these supposed transgressions. These negotiations are similar to those in other precarious settings, such as those of Tamil and Muslim women in post-conflict Sri Lanka who contest caste and gender expectations and power hierarchies as a way of gaining 'spaces of economic agency' (Rajasingham-Senanayake 2006: 178). Women like Khushida are able to use the instability brought about by life in the camps to negotiate new possibilities for themselves.

However, traditional notions of morality and honour – *izzot* – continue to condition notions of gender identity within the camps and whether Rohingya women are able to partake in NGO activities, particularly workshops and trainings. To maintain the respect and social reputation of one's family is akin to maintaining honour in the community (Baxter 2007: 745). A woman's ability to engage in such aspects of camp life is often influenced – and curtailed – by the perceived threat of public shaming as well as threats to the family honour, which could lead to reputational damage. I noticed there was a stark difference in the way paid work was viewed as opposed to participation in NGO trainings and workshops. Whereas, on the one hand, it was generally somewhat acceptable for Rohingya women in the camps to engage in paid employment (whether at home or with NGOs) given the changing gender divisions of labour in the camp and growing unemployment among men, there was significantly greater concern amongst men of the prevalence of gender rights discourse used by NGOs that seemingly gave women more authority and preference over men. Many men were weary of the UN's role beyond simply providing food rations and other essential services. Kader Imam (the *huzur* introduced in Chapter 5) was particularly blunt in his criticism of the UN and NGOs, as he told me:

> We were happy with UN support for food rations, but now with all these workshops they are running ... especially the ones for women. Those are not necessary. They are involving themselves in our family affairs. Before we [local elders and *huzurs*] were in charge of helping to fix any issues that arise in the community – especially family problems and things like that. Now when there is a problem, women do not call us to help them. They only go to the workshops.

Kader Imam's remarks reveal that while the NGOs, the UN, and other aid agencies were helpful in the initial setting up and ration support refugees got, as the months progressed, these organizations' provision of more skills-based trainings, workshops, and access to opportunities created ideological tensions as they were largely perceived by Rohingya men as targeted against their interests. Rohingya men felt further emasculation due to the UN's involvement in 'family affairs', in addition to their already weakened economic contribution to the household. Men's power and authority over women was further deteriorating with women's new 'bargaining power' as a result of the various gender trainings and workshops. Kader Imam's statement also conveyed a sense of nostalgia for the way things used to be in the past in Myanmar, when NGOs were not involved in Rohingya affairs. NGO involvement, from Kader Imam's statement, alluded to a form of transformation that was perhaps 'too forward' in giving women opportunities that he felt were not in line with traditional understandings of Rohingya culture and societal expectations for women. His sentiments were echoed by many men throughout the camps who were now having to navigate these new cultural shifts in mindsets.

In a similar vein, while some women embraced the Western notion of 'human rights' advocated by NGOs, others contended that men and women had different yet complementary roles and thus should be given different rights and responsibilities according to their sex. When we were returning back to her shelter from a workshop one evening, another frequent participant in NGO workshops, 18-year-old Fahmida, told me that she has to 'walk a fine line' because of the traditional mindset of not just Rohingya men but also Rohingya women. She said:

> When the NGOs tell me to encourage other women to join the workshops, I am happy to do it. In fact, I am proud of the changes I am seeing in myself. It is important to learn about these things. But we have to be careful how we talk to men. Perhaps others are more confident than me and are comfortable to take a leading position – like Khushida – she is able to talk in front of the men and express her opinion. I am the same age as Khushida but I am more comfortable to be quiet and allow the men to speak because it is more respectful in our culture to do so. I am making small changes in my family with the knowledge the workshop is giving me. But it is more honourable to do what is appropriate in our culture and religion. I don't want to do something that will be different from Rohingya customs.

Fahmida remarked that NGOs had a tendency to introduce ideas that did not necessarily coincide well with Rohingya culture and conceptions of appropriate Islamic behaviour, and thus while she agreed there was a need for more awareness of women's rights she did not believe in abandoning more traditional gendered roles that were given to men and women. In this manner, there was a constant shaping of her gendered identities – unlike Khushida's supposed ability to 'transgress' gender norms and ideologies, which gives her the ability to manoeuvre and gain power – Fahmida chose to work *within* the gendered boundaries of her culture. Women like Fahmida seek to reconcile knowledge gained through NGOs with Rohingya cultural norms – norms which she herself ascribes to. These constant negotiations surrounding acceptable cultural practices entailed subtle yet perceptible transformations that allowed women like Fahmida to find a 'middle ground' between traditional gender roles and newly introduced ideologies and concepts within the camps. This required limiting the 'rights' discourse at times – particularly when it could lead to a potential conflict – and instead asserting it in a way that could sway or incrementally adjust existing traditions without undermining them.

The *Majhee* System and 'Empowering' Women

The language of 'empowerment' was not necessarily received well by all in the camp. Some of my interlocutors felt that NGO workshops sought a particular goal, but in many cases, they neither improved the social position of women within their communities nor provided them with avenues to utilize and implement the skills they learned into their everyday lives. Khushida once told me that while the workshops do provide important skills and knowledge that most Rohingya women do not have access to in Myanmar, she was concerned about 'how can we implement these things when our society is still run by men with little input from women'. It was a poignant question and touched on a larger issue surrounding the prospect of 'empowerment', given that the entire administrative system at the Kutupalong–Balukhali mega-camp was run through *majhee*s.

NGOs rely heavily on *majhee*s to do the main legwork for any programming they undertake. As briefly outlined in Chapter 4, the *majhee* system was established by the Bangladeshi authorities – particularly the Bangladeshi army – as an emergency response arrangement due to the sudden influx of Rohingyas arriving at the country. Because of the immense challenges of overseeing more than a million refugees – all of whom arrived in just a few weeks – the *majhee* system, even if imperfect, can be viewed as a means of creating some sense of order through hierarchy, thereby facilitating the Bangladeshi government's efforts to manage the camps. A *majhee*'s primary tasks involve identifying the immediate survival needs of the particular zone they administer, linking refugees with emergency assistance from various providers, and acting as an intermediary authority for NGO programming. The *majhee* system was not established with the participation of the Rohingya community and consequently lacks representation and accountability for the refugees. They are not traditional leaders, elders, or even necessarily respected members of the community – while some *majhee*s may perform their role dutifully, others are highly suspect as they prioritize personal interests over that of the community. The *majhee* system certainly does not reflect the age and gender composition of the Rohingya refugee population, which includes almost exclusively middle-aged men.

Refugees must receive permission from their respective zone *majhee* for such activities as getting married, accessing relief items distributed by various NGOs, and especially, access to resources for social and mental health support. Aid organizations rely heavily on *majhee*s to distribute humanitarian aid, including food packages and other relief items. One aid worker told me nonchalantly that 'this is way things are'. He continued:

> It's an excellent system. It works very well because we can outsource the difficult work of having to choose who to properly distribute the items to. *Majhee*s also report to us if there are any specific issues in their zone such as gender-based violence or any other such troubles. They're trustworthy people for the most part and make our job more efficient. I couldn't imagine having to do this work without their cooperation.

This comment resonated amongst a variety of aid workers I spoke to who may have had some criticisms of the *majhee* system but for the most part felt that the culture in the camps would have been 'too difficult to navigate if not for the *majhee*s', as noted by an NGO staff member. Nonetheless, the heavy reliance on the discourse of 'empowerment' that humanitarian aid agencies propagate through their programming has been received with great scepticism by Rohingya women as the *majhee* system works in direct opposition to the ideals that they are being taught. Momtaz Khatun explained this contradiction succinctly when she told me in a hushed voice, even as we sat inside her shelter out of fear that someone may hear her:

> *Majhee*s are all frauds. We have to inform them of everything and they are always checking up on us. I went to one of those NGO workshops where they tell us about those types of things [referring to 'empowerment' and 'rights'] but how can we even use these things when they themselves are abusing the system by setting up these *majhee*s. All the *majhee*s are here only for money. If we have any problems, first we need to give them money and then they think if they want to help us – that thinking phase will take another few months. As you know in our culture women do not share things – only with other women we do – but why will go to these *majhee*s and share our problems when we know

they will not do anything? One time I heard a woman who was getting beaten by her husband a lot, so she told the *majhee* to fix the matter and involve the authorities. The *majhee* said he will do it, but it is now already three months and nobody has done anything. The man is still beating his wife.

Momtaz Khatun's concerns clearly reveals that whether, and how, a case is reported to the camp authorities is fully contingent on the *majhee*. Jeanne Ward and Beth Vann (2002) in their study on gender-based violence in refugee settings, particularly Tanzania, suggest that the needs of women and justice are often filtered through elders. Although the UNHCR and other aid organizations have set up centres within the Kutupalong–Balukhali mega-camp for women and men to share their experiences, these centres are only very sparingly used by Rohingya women, partly because of the stigma associated with sexual and gender-based violence but also because the power structure created through the *majhee* system, which makes it difficult to discuss such sensitive matters outside the family. Women are often referred to as the *majhee* in the first instance, who are then supposed to facilitate a type of 'reconciliation' amongst a fighting couple, for example. Thus, the language of 'empowerment' rings hollow for many of my interlocutors, who felt that the hierarchical nature of the *majhee* system and the NGO community that relies on it at the expense of their well-being does not necessarily give them bargaining power within their families. While Rohingya women are being taught on the one hand to shift their identities by using the tool of 'empowerment', NGOs deference to the authority of *majhee*s in fact only works to cement tensions on people's ideals of masculinity and femininity. Gender ideologies and distinctions continue to persist, which are only brought more clearly to light through the efforts of humanitarian aid agencies that advocate for women's empowerment.

In this vein, El-Bushra (2004: 261) suggests that '[interventions] aimed at taking advantage of rapid change in conflict and post-conflict situations to encourage transformations in gender relations ... [are] unrealistic'. In most contexts, the *majhee*s usually defer decision-making to the male head of the family – even if the woman is the breadwinner. This deference conforms to the existing social order and thus not only fits with the 'normal' course of events but also protects the *majhee*'s own interests as he is viewed as maintaining the existing social hierarchy that privileges men. Some of my interlocutors felt slighted by *majhee*s for not including them in important decision-making matters, while others agreed that their husbands should have the final say after discussing with the *majhee*. But even in those cases, many women felt that they would prefer to have an opinion, even if it was not the final opinion. Having to constantly deal with the gender hierarchical system of the *majhee* affected Rohingya women's gendered subjectivities. My interlocutors often ended up confused with this and found it 'hypocritical' – as suggested by Zomila – who thought the illusion of gender equality had more negative effects in their society than positive.

Navigating Humanitarian Power Dynamics

The preceding discussion was related to a larger issue of the humanitarian aid landscape in the camps, which I found was a common feeling amongst most of my interlocutors. One evening after the *taleem*, as Zomila and I shared some tea and biscuits, a woman walked by Zomila's shelter and stopped to chat with us. Before leaving, she encouraged Zomila to attend an upcoming workshop run by a local NGO. I noticed that Zomila scoffed at the woman's suggestion and said to her, in an almost shouting manner: 'Ay! We've just finished *Allah'r kam* (God's work) and you are talking about these useless matters!' The lady took it lightly, flicked the side of her shawl, smiled at Zomila, and walked off into the hot sun. When I later asked Zomila what she meant by her statement to the other woman – if anything at all – her answer was revealing:

> Let me tell you, I started this *taleem* because of these NGOs. They are always involving themselves in our business and now women are going off to these programmes where they do sewing and other things. Why? When we were in Myanmar we didn't need all these things. We always used to do *taleem*s – we were happy like that. Sometimes I see these women and I ask them if the workshops they attend are helpful, and most of the time they have nothing to say. They say that the NGOs are paying them some small amount to participate in the workshop and then they go back to their shelters. How many of these organizations are sitting with us? How many have come to our *taleem* and see how we do things according to our culture and religion? It is important to discuss things according to our Islamic way. Did these NGOs come anytime to ask us how it is done in our religion? Barely any of them. They come, think we are all living terrible lives – yes, we have many problems – but we are also able to do many things. *Taleem*s are run by Rohingya women. How is that not empowerment? These groups say that only the NGOs' work is empowering for us Rohingya women. But if you ask any woman that goes to the *taleem*, she will tell you that our religion is giving us more empowerment than what they can offer. This is why more women are joining our *taleem*s than they are joining those workshops.

Zomila's comments were indicative of the larger issues surrounding humanitarian aid agencies working in refugee settings. Expanding on the discussion noted in Chapter 4 on *taleem*s, Zomila's narrative emphasizes the failure of aid agencies to view refugee women as more than simply 'bare life'. At one point, Tafura (introduced in Chapter 5) stopped by Zomila's shelter as we spoke, and she too joined our discussion. She told me that she had participated in the safety workshop a few weeks prior but decided not to go to others that were upcoming, echoing Zomila's statements. Her criticisms were more pointed, and she explained to me that when most of these workshops are led, they are usually accompanied by handouts with information that they can take back to their families and community to share. This is a point of embarrassment for most of my interlocutors as the majority of Rohingya women are illiterate. Tafura sighed in frustration as she recounted her experience:

> I didn't like it one bit. The people who are running these know we cannot read. How can we take these handouts – what will we do with them? If we show our husbands that 'this is what we learned' and ask him to read it, he will just throw it away and say it is useless. Only handful of Rohingya women know how to read. Even amongst the youth there are not many girls that can read. So what will we do with these sheets? Some of the discussions we had in the class were good, but it feels like a lot of show. These foreigners they come in, we show our face for a few minutes, and then they go away for good. We never see them again. They like to include women because it helps them, but nobody is listening to our concerns. Most of us are there only for show. So what is the point of wasting time to go to these workshops? Better I should come to the *taleem* and make *du'a* and reflect on Allah's teachings and teach my kids that.

Tafura's complaints were common amongst the vast majority of my interlocutors. While some of my interlocutors feel there are some positive aspects to NGO programming, there is general disinterest in participation, as many feel they are being used as pawns in a larger scheme – what Szczepaniková (2008) suggests are 'reiterative performances' where NGOs use this 'feminization' of refugees to create an illusion of gender equality and balance in their programming while ignoring the real concerns of the refugees. There was a general feeling amongst many of my interlocutors who repeatedly spoke of the 'performative' aspect of NGO interactions – where the image of victimhood was nurtured and enacted in a way that was exploitative. Jennifer Hyndman and Malathi De Alwis (2003) suggest that this is indicative of humanitarianism and the way humanitarian aid agencies operate, where specific 'scripts' must be followed. Zannat also had a few interactions with NGOs and found the exploitative nature of them particularly appalling, telling me:

> These NGOs are always burdening us – asking us for pictures. They just tell us to stand in one place or the other like we are a bunch of sheep being herded. It feels bad to always be used like this – always asking for help. We are refugees, but before that we are people. Sometimes I feel that the world has forgotten that we also have our boundaries and what is okay or not okay. But not so many people ask us what we are comfortable with. The *majhee* will just bring a bunch of us together if the NGO asks him to – so we go and we say what needs to be said. And also, they only want to hear our sad stories. There are many sad stories – every family here has so many stories – but nobody is asking about our dreams and goals. Sometimes they see us as women who are always only sad. But we want to talk about what we hope for, not only what we lost.

Zannat poignantly narrated her ambivalent feelings about being used like 'sheep' by NGOs for their own gain. Her narrative also revealed the way 'sad' stories are employed by NGOs as a form of what Ong (2003: 14) calls 'systems of female clientship'. Szczepaniková (2008) goes on to argue that refugees are often seen as 'clients' as a way to self-promote NGO activity. These hit on issues that have long plagued the humanitarian industry, of oversimplified narratives showing a one-dimensional picture of the refugees' lives – particularly women's lives.

My interlocutors were often struck when I asked them about their lives beyond simply the hardships and struggles they faced – and in most cases, they excitedly wanted to share more about the other aspects of their life. Zannat's suggestion that 'nobody is asking about our dreams and goals' is a lucid illustration of the flattening of refugee experiences instead of presenting them with complexity. To this end, Lila Abu-Lughod (2013: 78) succinctly notes that 'superficial vignettes and extreme cases tell us little about the variety of ways women experience their lives and the contexts we must appreciate in order to make sense of their suffering'. In many ways my interlocutors were challenging the notion of being seen as the 'sad third world Muslim woman' under a 'womenandchildren' trope, which only 'flattens [their] three-dimensional lives' without properly explaining the wider context of their stories (Enloe 1991). As this apolitical 'womenandchildren' group, women like Zannat feel that they are deprived of complexity and are simply abstracted into the image of a 'sad, hopeless' woman. Zannat nonetheless feels that given the gender order in her household, she is compelled to do these favours to NGOs as it provides support for her family.

But this was not to say that Rohingya women were not negotiating their femininity and using their image to strengthen their networks with NGOs and increase their sympathizers as a way of capitalizing on the opportunities that come with participating in NGO activities. Hamida told me how she had a more positive view of NGOs, not only because she worked with an NGO-run co-operative but also because she felt that she better understood how to 'work the system', as she told me. I sat with her and a few friends as we cut vegetables one morning before she left for the day, and when the topic of NGO assistance came up, she said:

> *Afa*, what can I tell you? The truth is that we have to be very strategic – and I am always telling these women [*pointing to the other ladies*] – we are now in the system and at the mercy of these NGOs. They are here to help us. So we need to learn how to make use of them. I work with these foreigners sometimes, so I know what they want. They want lots of pictures of women being sad or doing some type of activity because then it helps them to promote their work. And in turn they give me more opportunities – like I got the job with the NGO because I always used to join them for their pictures. Whenever they wanted to take pictures, I would tell my *majhee* that they should pick me. I went more and more to these picture sessions and then the NGO people got to know me and now look, *Allah'r shokr*, I now have this job. And even other times when we participate we get some extra money or food packs – sometimes they give us different types of gifts. You know that nice pink shawl I showed you the other day? One of the nice foreigner women gave it to me. So this way we have to learn to make use of the system that we are living in. I don't think there is anything wrong in doing this.

Hamida's remarks reveal the complex manner in which Rohingya women have been able to assert agency within a system that they vitally depend on for survival and that from the outside seems to provide little room to navigate. Some women have become fed up with the expectations of 'reciprocity' that involves NGOs and refugees as their 'clients'. However, other women like Hamida have been able to use their knowledge of the running of these NGOs and their interests to strategically position themselves as ideal 'subjects' who exhibit the success of their programmatic efforts. These 'performances' allow Rohingya women to access even greater resources, and they come to be viewed as 'trusted clients' who can be relied upon to demonstrate the success of

NGO efforts (Szczepaniková 2008). In this way, Hamida was able to negotiate her gendered identity in a way that positioned her favourably, thereby allowing her to recapture agency.

Conclusion

The presence of the international humanitarian aid community within the camps introduced Rohingyas to initiatives, programming, and opportunities that they were previously not exposed to. NGOs organized workshops on 'women's empowerment' and trainings on gender-based violence – a substantial number of women were being included in these activities, which would not have been fathomable in the past. Participating in these activities requires Rohingya women to strategically negotiate around the expectations of male community leaders on notions of 'honour' and *purdah* that are central elements of Rohingya culture.

While, on the one hand, NGOs and aid agencies speak the language of 'empowerment', these NGOs also heavily rely on the *majhee* system to be able to carry out community projects. The over-reliance of NGOs on male community leaders – *majhee*s – posed particular challenges for Rohingya women, as it served to further legitimize and solidify the existing patriarchal hierarchies that the language of 'empowerment' sought to deconstruct. Furthermore, NGOs often deploy expected gender norms of masculinity and femininity alongside images of vulnerability and victimhood to achieve particular goals. While some women embrace and negotiate their gendered identity to benefit from the humanitarian system, others feel like 'pawns' in a larger scheme. These various gendered dynamics highlight the ways in which 'gender programming' directly impacts and transforms gender dynamics within the camps.

8

Conclusion

Through the narratives of everyday experiences, I have sought to examine the transformation of gender identity, relations, and roles of Rohingya women in the refugee camps in Bangladesh – of how they see themselves and how they *make a life* despite their difficult circumstances. Focusing on the voices of Rohingya women helps to highlight the impacts of forced migration on how the 'gendered self is transformed' and the ways in which these women learn to negotiate and navigate new environments, thereby reshaping 'strategies of selfhood' (Bhabha 1994; Abusharaf 2009; Fiddian-Qasmiyeh 2014). While the prevailing scholarly literature on refugees details many of the complexities of displacement, much of the attention is put on the challenges and suffering faced by refugees during and after forced migration. One strand of research that remains underrepresented is a grounded understanding of refugee experiences more broadly – and that of refugee women specifically – that focuses on their ability to reconstruct their lives after displacement. This book is an attempt to look beyond these broad assumptions by providing a lens into the *everyday*, the *mundane*, the *quotidian* parts of Rohingya women's lives in the Kutupalong–Balukhali mega-camp, after experiencing violence and forced migration. Through the narratives, stories, and emotions conveyed in the preceding chapters, I have sought to uncover how the experiences of Rohingya women during and after forced migration, as well as their strategic deployment of varying forms and degrees of economic, social, and cultural capital, help them to recreate a sense of community and 'life' in the camps. This book thus showcases the creative capacity of refugee women to apply their own frames of meaning within the camps – frames that are distinct from the commonly promoted or taken-for-granted assumptions of NGOs and humanitarian aid agencies.

Through feminist ethnographic research, this book has shown that the camps have neither destroyed pre-existing conceptions of masculinity and femininity, nor have they left them unchanged – instead, these notions have come to occupy an 'in-between' space, opening up the possibilities of empowerment while also reifying gendered expectations. Gendered positions do not remain static – rather, Rohingya women negotiate and navigate patriarchal structures and power asymmetries, highlighting their agentic capacity. This was evident in the recreation of the *taleem*, which was borne out of Rohingya women's desire for social continuity in the way 'home' was reimagined through bonding, kinship, and social organization. Rohingya women's recreation of the *taleem* in exile was, in its own way, a reflection of how their actions showed them to be more than mere victims. Rather, by creatively reshaping and reorganizing this physical and social space, they have become active social agents despite the limiting constraints on their lives. Their resilience becomes visible through their intense will to survive, thrive, and remain steadfast – all of which serve as a means of resisting their condition. Their actions do not take the form of outward or public resistance, but they nonetheless reveal an innovative and meaningful manner of catalysing social change through the memories, narratives, and meanings that shape their social world.

As countless Rohingyas lost many family members during periods of violence and displacement, marriage became a central means of recreating family bonds. Marriage was viewed as an opportunity for increased freedoms; however, this view was complicated by the increasing interest that women had in educational and other available opportunities within the camps. Issues of *mahr* and the wide prevalence of available unmarried women as opposed to the shortage of eligible, marriageable men, forced women to contend with issues surrounding their gendered identity. Furthermore, women had a constant desire to uphold the ideals of being a 'good girl' or an 'ideal wife' in the camps; upholding this fantasy required creativity – and even forbearance of violence – on their part as they sought to navigate new employment opportunities while their husbands remained jobless. Different women ascribed different meanings to their work; while some women challenged hegemonic normative gendered structures, others chose to – or felt the compulsion to – work within existing rules and gender hierarchies.

Aside from navigating new household and community dynamics, Rohingya women also face a host of expectations, challenges, and opportunities from the presence of the humanitarian aid industry in the refugee camps. Many of the gender programming efforts of NGOs and aid agencies had direct impacts on the gender asymmetries already present within the Rohingya community. The advent of 'gender equality' programming in the camps – particularly centred around the advocacy of 'women's empowerment' and the 'feminisation of the refugee clientele' (Szczepaniková 2008) – disrupted prevailing gender dynamics. The language of rights and women's empowerment exposed some of the prevailing gender hierarchies, at times calling them to question and at other times even undermining the position of men in the community. However, such advocacy efforts, on the one hand, were completely countered by the NGO and humanitarian community's reliance on the *majhee* system, while, on the other, enhanced the legitimacy afforded to this male-dominated system of organization in the camps, which had the unintended consequence of further constraining women. Women were expected to negotiate their femininity in order to strengthen their networks and capitalize on various opportunities available in the camps. In many ways, Rohingya women were having to challenge patriarchal structures while engaging in strategic choices and bargaining to rebuild their lives (Kandiyoti 1988).

In the end, I am only able to share one part of the Rohingya refugee story – that of the lives of a small group of women exiled in the Kutupalong–Balukhali mega-camp in Bangladesh. There are millions of other Rohingyas, all scattered across the globe. But the story I presented in this book is an important one, as it provides the initial groundwork on the gendered micro-dynamics at play in a rich site of inquiry through a long-term ethnographic approach, which has implications for further research on the Rohingya refugee crisis and forced migration studies more broadly. A more multi-sited comparative approach with Rohingya refugees settled in other countries would be a valuable project to reveal how gendered dynamics have transformed not only as a result of different geographic 'endpoints' but also due to varying institutional constraints – for example, camp versus city. Such an undertaking could offer a deeper understanding of why Rohingya women left Myanmar and travelled to certain destinations as opposed to others and the complex and varied reasons behind migration journeys – some women left behind their families and travelled alone, others chased husbands to Bangladesh, still others fled with their children in search of a new home but with no particular destination in mind. Such an inquiry would allow for an intricate narrative of migratory 'push and pull factors' to emerge, thus providing insights on how different endpoints have had different effects on the life that Rohingya women have made for themselves.

Reflections on Moving Forward

Since leaving fieldwork in late 2018, I have returned to the camps every few months to continue engagement with my interlocutors and have witnessed the camps changing with time and politics. After the 25 August 2017 attacks in Rakhine State, the Government of Bangladesh yielded to the mass exodus of Rohingyas and continued to keep its borders open to the influx of refugees, as it led the humanitarian response to the crisis. By keeping the borders open, Bangladesh received praise from the international community; however, the increasing difficulty of supporting so many refugees has resulted in increased efforts by the Bangladeshi government to repatriate Rohingya refugees back to Myanmar (Alam 2018; de Chickera 2018). As a result, as recently as March 2019, the Bangladesh government stated to the UN Security Council, for the first time, that they 'would no longer be in a position to accommodate more people from Myanmar', going on to express increased frustration at the lack of action from the international community and from Myanmar to develop concrete solutions to the crisis and a suitable process for repatriation (Ellis-Petersen 2018, 2019).

While these ever-shifting political dynamics play out on the international stage, Rohingya women are working every day to make a life for themselves in the refugee camps – the days go on, as there is cooking to be done, children to take care of, friends to talk to, ties to rekindle. There are smiles and joy and moments of peace and solace. And though my fieldwork has ended, friendship has not, and so we continue to sit together, eat together, cry together – I am still listening and learning.

The value in feminist research are the long-term bonds of trust that emerge between researchers and interlocutors – it has the capacity to reveal rich narratives of women's everyday lived experiences in a manner that is too often missing in scholarly, development, and humanitarian discourses on refugee women's lives. Throughout my time spent with my interlocutors, I found that they often did not use or participate in the various projects that humanitarian agencies had set up for them – such as women-friendly spaces. And thus, I have tried to *bear witness* to Rohingya women's struggles and to *listen* to *their* voices. Only by doing so can we hope to move scholarly discussions beyond monolithic treatments of refugee experiences in the camps – namely, one tainted by problems and hardships, and towards a more open-textured frame of analysis where women are active agents as opposed to passive recipients of the social dynamics that animate the camps. When Rohingya women are able to carve out spaces for themselves like the *taleem*, it is a reminder that they in fact have the answers to some of the challenges they face. It is thus necessary for scholarly discussions to appreciate the value of listening to Rohingya refugee women's voices, and recognizing their *own* and *active* efforts at rebuilding their lives and their social worlds. Only then can we move beyond simplistic notions of Rohingya women as 'helpless' and devoid of agency toward an understanding that views them as creative, inventive beings.

Epilogue

I end this book by returning to the beginning. Throughout my fieldwork, I thought of Rahima often and reflected on her haunting description of 'floating through life'. *How is she doing now? Did she still feel like she was floating? What did she really mean by 'we will only keep floating until the day we die'?* I wanted so terribly to ask her these questions the next time we planned to meet. But I never got the chance. Less than three weeks after our first meeting on that hot summer evening in August 2017, Rahima passed away. Nobody was able to tell for sure how or what the reason was. Some say it was due to a sudden fever and diarrhoea; others say it was because of unbearable grief after learning that her husband was murdered by the Myanmar army while in jail.

There is death in the Rohingya refugee camps – a lot of it. I intentionally did not dwell on death in this book as I wanted to focus on *life* – life that is messy and difficult and filled with immense pain, though nonetheless hopeful and resilient despite all odds. But as hard as she tried to remain hopeful for her children, it was not enough for Rahima. I pray that she has finally reached the shores.

Glossary

abiyata mayya-fua	unmarried girl
adhan	call to prayer
afa	a respectful term meaning 'big sister'
akth	solemnization of marriage
alima	learned person, or teacher (female)
Allah'r shokr	thanks to Allah
azadi	freedom
bazu	dress
beshi biya	polygamy
bhalo mayya-fua	good girl
bhasha-manush	'floating' people
biya-shaadi	marriage
burqa	full body and face veil
CNG	auto-rickshaw
daal	lentil
dhikr	remembrance of God by reciting short prayers
du'a	supplication
dukkho	sadness
hadiat	gift
hariken	kerosene lamp
huzur	local imam
inshaAllah	God willing
Isha	the night prayer
izzot	honour or social reputation
izzotdar	respectable family; families with *izzot*
Jumu'ah	Friday afternoon congregational prayer
khala	aunt

khalamma	elderly aunt – usually used as a sign of respect for elderly women
lungi	a type of sarong in South Asia worn only by men
Maghrib	the evening prayer
mahr	Islamic gift to the bride from the groom
majhee	individual heads of zones in the refugee camps
manosh'sha biya	promised marriage
Mog	the Rakhine people in Myanmar
mehndi	henna
panjabi	traditional shirt and pant outfit (sometimes refers only to the shirt)
para	settlement
Qiyamat	Day of Judgement
takoth sara mayya-fua	vulnerable women
taleem	a gathering for prayer, supplication, and study of the Qur'an
tarana	Rohingya songs
thanaka	a yellow-paste makeup native to Myanmar
tomtom	auto-rickshaw
tupi	a rounded skullcap often worn for prayer
yaba	drugs
zulm	oppression, also used interchangeably to mean rape – the official word for rape is *bolazuri zulm*, though most people simply use *zulm*

Bibliography

Abu-Lughod, L. (1990). 'The Romance of Resistance: Tracing Transformations of Power through Bedouin Women'. *American Ethnologist* 17 (1): 41–55.

———. (2002). 'Do Muslim Women Really Need Saving? Anthropological Reflections on Cultural Relativism and Its Others'. *American Anthropologist* 104 (3): 783–790.

———. (2013). *Do Muslim Women Need Saving?* Massachusetts: Harvard University Press.

Abusharaf, R. M. (2005). 'Smoke Bath: Renegotiating Self and the World in a Sudanese Shantytown'. *Anthropology and Humanism* 30 (1): 1–21.

———. (2009). *Transforming Displaced Women in Sudan: Politics and the Body in a Squatter Settlement.* Chicago: University of Chicago Press.

Adams, H., S. Ghanem, and M. Collins. (2018). *Same Space, Different Places: How Bonds to Place Affect Well-Being and Social-Cohesion in Syrian Refugees and Their Lebanese Host Communities.* The British Academy. https://www.kcl.ac.uk/geography/assets/helen-adams-m%C3%A1ir%C3%A9ad-collins-and-samar-ghanem-2018-same-space-different-places-how-bonds-to-place-affect-well-being-and-social-cohesion-in-syrian-refugees-and-their-lebanese-host-communities-english-version.pdf. Accessed 12 December 2018.

Adler, P. A. and P. Adler. (1994). 'Observational Techniques'. In *Handbook of Qualitative Research*, edited by K. N. Denzin and S. Y. Lincoln, 377–392. London: Sage Publications.

Agamben, G. (1998). *Homo Sacer: Sovereign Power and Bare Life.* Stanford: Stanford University Press.

Agger, I. (1992). *The Blue Room: Trauma and Testimony Among Refugee Women.* London: Zed Books.

Agier, M. (2011). *Managing the Undesirables: Refugee Camps and Humanitarian Government.* Cambridge: Polity Press.

———. (2014). 'Introduction: L'encampement du Monde'. In *Un Monde de Camps*, edited by M. Agier, 11–29. Paris: La Découverte.

Ahmed, A. S. (1992). *Postmodernism and Islam: Predicament and Promise*. London: Routledge.

Akhter, S. and K. Kusakabe. (2014). 'Gender-Based Violence among Documented Rohingya Refugees in Bangladesh'. *Indian Journal of Gender Studies* 21 (2): 225–246.

Alam, M. (2018). 'Enduring Entanglement: The Multi-Sectoral Impact of the Rohingya Crisis on Neighboring Bangladesh'. *Georgetown Journal of International Affairs* 19: 20–26.

Albert, E. (2017). 'The Rohingya Migrant Crisis'. Council on Foreign Relations. https://ethz.ch/content/dam/ethz/special-interest/gess/cis/center-for-securities-studies/resources/docs/CFR_The%20Rohingya%20Migrant%20Crisis%20-%20Council%20on%20Foreign%20Relations.pdf. Accessed 13 January 2017.

Al Jazeera. (2016). 'Rohingya Face Myanmar "Ethnic Cleansing": UN Official'. http://www.aljazeera.com/news/2016/11/rohingya-face-myanmar-ethnic-cleansing-official-161125065731036.html. Accessed 13 January 2017.

Altorki, S. and C. El-Solh (eds.). (1988). *Studying Your Own Society: Arab Women in the Field*. Cairo: American University of Cairo Press.

Appadurai, A. (1996). *Modernity at Large: Cultural Dimensions of Globalization*. Minneapolis: University of Minnesota Press.

Arendt, H. (1968). *Men in Dark Times*. New York: Harcourt.

Bartolomei, L., E. Pittaway, and E. E. Pittaway. (2003). 'Who Am I? Identity and Citizenship in Kakuma Refugee Camp in Northern Kenya'. *Development* 46: 87–94.

Bateson, M. C. (1989). *Composing a Life*. New York: Grove Press.

Baxter, D. (2007). 'Honor Thy Sister: Selfhood, Gender, and Agency in Palestinian Culture'. *Anthropological Quarterly* 80 (3): 737–775.

Becker, G. (1994). 'Metaphors in Disrupted Lives: Infertility and Cultural Constructions of Continuity'. *Medical Anthropology Quarterly* 8 (4): 383–410.

Behar, R. and D. A. Gordon (eds.). (1995). *Women Writing Culture*. Berkeley: University of California Press.

Bernard, H. R. (2013). *Social Research Methods: Qualitative and Quantitative Approaches*. Thousand Oaks: Sage Publications.

Bhabha, H. K. (1994). *The Location of Culture*. London: Routledge.

Bhattacharya, B. (1927). 'Bengali Influence in Arakan, Bengal Past and Present'. *Journal of the Calcutta Historical Society* 33 (65–66): 139–144.

Bhatia, A., A. Mahmud, A. Fuller, R. Shin, T. Shatil, M. Sultana, K. A. M. Morshed, J. Leaning, and S. Balsari. (2018). 'The Rohingya in Cox's Bazar: When the Stateless Seek Refuge'. *Health and Human Rights* 20 (2): 105–122.

Blomquist, R. (2016). 'Ethno-Demographic Dynamics of the Rohingya–Buddhist Conflict'. Master's thesis, Georgetown University.

Bourdieu, P. (1977). *Outline of a Theory of Practice*. Cambridge: Cambridge University Press.

Brun, C. (2000). 'Making Young Displaced Men Visible'. *Forced Migration Review* 9 (December): 10–12.

Bryman, A. (2008). *Social Research Methods*. 3rd ed. New York: New York University Press.

Burnett, A. and P. Michael. (2001). 'Health Needs of Asylum Seekers and Refugees'. *British Medical Journal* 322 (7285): 544–547.

Butler, J. (1998). 'Sex and Gender in Simone de Beauvoir's Second Sex'. In *Simone de Beauvoir: A Critical Reader*, edited by E. Fallaize, 35–49. New York: Routledge.

Callamard, A. (1996). 'Flour Is Power: The Gendered Division of Labour in Lisongwe Camp'. In *Development and Diaspora: Gender and the Refugee Experience*, edited by W. M. Giles, P. Van Esterik, and H. Moussa, 176–198. Dundas: Artemis.

Carr, E. and A. Worth (2001). 'The Use of the Telephone Interview for Research'. *Journal of Research in Nursing* 6 (1): 511–524.

Cernea, M. M. (2000). 'Risks, Safeguards, and Reconstruction: A Model for Population Displacement and Resettlement'. In *Risks and Reconstruction: Experiences of Resettlers and Refugees*, edited by M. M. Cernea and C. N. W. McDowell, 11–55. Washington: The World Bank.

Cerwonka, A. and L. Malkki. (2007). *Improvising Theory: Process and Temporality in Ethnographic Fieldwork*. Chicago: University of Chicago Press.

Chan, E. Y. Y., C. P. Chiu, and G. K. W. Chan. (2018). 'Medical and Health Risks Associated with Communicable Diseases of Rohingya Refugees in Bangladesh 2017'. *International Journal of Infectious Diseases* 68 (January): 39–43.

Chatty, D. (2014). 'Anthropology and Forced Migration'. In *The Oxford Handbook of Refugee and Forced Migration Studies*, edited by E. Fiddian-Qasmiyeh, G. Loescher, K. Long, and N. Sigona, 7–85. Oxford: Oxford University Press.

Clark, N. (2017). 'The Unspeakable Horrors Endured by the World's Most Persecuted Minority'. *Vice*. https://www.vice.com/en/article/gyxvv9/

myanmar-burma-rohingya-worlds-most-persecuted-minority. Accessed 11 March 2017.

Cockburn, C. (1998). *The Space Between Us: Negotiating Gender and National Identities in Conflict*. New York: Zed Books.

Colson, E. (1999). 'Gendering Those Uprooted by Development'. In *Engendering Forced Migration: Theory and Practice*, edited by D. Indra, 23–39. New York: Berghahn.

———. (2003). 'Forced Migration and the Anthropological Response'. *Journal of Refugee Studies* 16 (1): 1–18.

Corbet, A. (2016). 'Community After All? An Inside Perspective on Encampment in Haiti'. *Journal of Refugee Studies* 29 (2): 166–186.

Coyle, D. and M. A. Jainul. (2020). 'Honour in Transition: Changing Gender Norms Among the Rohingya'. *Āarar Dilor Hota* (Voices of Our Hearts) Series. Bangladesh: IOM.

Crisol, C. (2001). 'Gender and Social Transformation'. *Philippine Sociological Review* 49 (January–December): 105–116.

Cross, J. E. (2015). 'Processes of Place Attachment: An Interactional Framework'. *Symbolic Interaction* 38 (4): 493–520.

Crossa, V. (2012). 'Relational Positionality: Conceptualizing Research, Power, and the Everyday Politics of Neoliberalization in Mexico City'. *ACME: An International E-Journal for Critical Geographies* 11 (1): 110–132.

Culcasi, K. (2019). '"We Are Women and Men Now": Intimate Spaces and Coping Labour for Syrian Women Refugees in Jordan'. *Transactions of the Institute of British Geographers* 44 (3): 463–478.

Daley, P. (1991). 'Gender, Displacement, and Social Reproduction: Settling Burundi Refugees in Western Tanzania'. *Journal of Refugee Studies* 4 (3): 248–266.

Davis, D. and C. Craven (2016). *Feminist Ethnography: Thinking Through Methodologies, Challenges, and Possibilities*. London: Rowman & Littlefield.

D'Costa, B. (2018). 'Of Responsibilities, Protection, and Rights: Children's Lives in Conflict Zones'. *Global Responsibility to Protect* 10 (1–2): 261–277.

de Beauvoir, S. (1988 [1953]). *The Second Sex*. London: Picador.

de Chickera, A. (2018). 'Statelessness and Identity in the Rohingya Refugee Crisis'. *Humanitarian Exchange* 73 (October): 7–10.

Denzin, N. K. (2009). *The Research Act: A Theoretical Introduction to Sociological Methods*. New York: Routledge.

Denzin, N. K. and Y. S. Lincoln (eds.). (2003). *Collecting and Interpreting Qualitative Materials*. London: Sage Publications.

Domínguez, G. (2015). 'Pushed Back – Malaysia Refuses Safe Haven to Abandoned Refugees'. *DW*. http://www.dw.com/en/pushed-back-malaysia-refuses-safe-haven-to-abandoned-refugees/a-18448132. Accessed 23 February 2017.

Dyck, I. and P. Dossa (2007). 'Place, Health and Home: Gender and Migration in the Constitution of Healthy Space'. *Health and Place* 13 (3): 691–701.

Eastmond, M. (2007). 'Stories as Lived Experience: Narratives in Forced Migration Research'. *Journal of Refugee Studies* 20 (2): 248–264.

Edward, J. K. (2007). *Sudanese Women Refugees: Transformations and Future Imaginings*. New York: Palgrave Macmillan.

Eisenbruch, M. (1991). 'From Post-Traumatic Stress Disorder to Cultural Bereavement: Diagnosis of Southeast Asian Refugees'. *Social Sciences and Medicine* 33 (6): 673–680.

El-Bushra, J. (2000). 'Transforming Conflict: Some Thoughts on a Gendered Understanding of Conflict Processes'. In *States of Conflict: Gender, Violence and Resistance*, edited by S. Jacobs, R. Jacobsen, and J. Marchbank, 66–86. London: Zed Books.

———. (2004). 'Fused in Combat: Gender Relations and Armed Conflict'. In *Development, Women, and War: Feminist Perspectives*, edited by H. Afshar and D. Eade, 152–171. Oxford: Oxfam GB.

El Jack, A. (2003). 'Cutting Edge Pack Series – Gender and Armed Conflict: Overview Report'. BRIDGE, Institute of Development Studies, University of Sussex. http://www.bridge.ids.ac.uk/bridge-publications/cutting-edge-packs/gender-and-armed-conflict. Accessed 23 February 2017.

———. (2008). 'In the Name of Development: Conflict, Displacement and Gender Transformation in Sudan'. PhD dissertation, York University.

Ellis-Petersen, H. (2018). 'UN Criticises Rohingya Deal between Myanmar and Bangladesh'. *The Guardian*, 31 October. https://www.theguardian.com/world/2018/oct/31/un-criticises-rohingya-deal-between-myanmar-and-bangladesh. Accessed 31 October 2018.

———. (2019). 'Rohingya Crisis: Bangladesh Says It Will Not Accept Any More Myanmar Refugees'. *The Guardian*, 1 March. https://www.theguardian.com/world/2019/mar/01/rohingya-crisis-bangladesh-says-it-will-not-accept-any-more-myanmar-refugees. Accessed 1 March 2019.

Elrashidi, M. N. (2005). 'Palestinian Women Under Occupation: Basic Analysis of their Status'. *MIFTAH*. http://www.miftah.org/Display.cfm?DocId=7966&CategoryId=21. Accessed 15 September 2018.

Elson, D. (1996). 'Male Bias in the Development Process: An Overview'. In *Male Bias in the Development Process*, edited by D. Elson, 1–28. Manchester: Manchester University Press.

Emerson, R. M., R. I. Fretz, and L. L. Shaw. (2011). *Writing Ethnographic Fieldnotes*. Chicago: The University of Chicago Press.

Enloe, C. H. (1991). '"Womenandchildren": Propaganda Tools of Patriarchy'. In *Mobilising Democracy: Changing the US Role in the Middle East*, edited by G. Bates, 89–96. Monroe: Common Courage Press.

Equal Rights Trust. (2014). *Equal Only in Name: The Human Rights of Stateless Rohingya in Malaysia*. The Institute of Human Rights and Peace Studies, Mahidol University.

Erchak, G. M. (1992). *The Anthropology of Self and Behavior*. New Brunswick: Rutgers University Press.

Farzana, K. F. (2011). 'Music and Artistic Artefacts: Symbols of Rohingya Identity and Everyday Resistance in Borderlands'. *Austrian Journal of South-East Asian Studies* 4 (2): 215–236.

———. (2015). 'Boundaries in Shaping the Rohingya Identity and the Shifting Context of Borderland Politics'. *Studies in Ethnicity and Nationalism* 15 (2): 292–314.

———. (2017). *Memories of Burmese Rohingya Refugees: Contested Identity and Belonging*. New York: Palgrave Macmillan.

Ferree, M. M., J. Lorber, and B. B. Hess (eds.). (1999). *Revisioning Gender*. London: Sage Publications.

Fiddian-Qasmiyeh, E. (2014). 'Gender and Forced Migration'. In *The Oxford Handbook of Refugee and Forced Migration Studies*, edited by E. Fiddian-Qasmiyeh, 395–408. Oxford: Oxford University Press.

Fiddian-Qasmiyeh, E., G. Loescher, K. Long, and N. Sigona (eds.). (2014). *The Oxford Handbook of Refugee and Forced Migration Studies*. Oxford: Oxford University Press.

Fincham, K. (2010). 'The Construction of the Palestinian Girl'. *Girlhood Studies* 3 (1): 34–54.

Flax, J. (1990). 'Postmodernism and Gender Relations in Feminist Theory'. In *Feminism/Postmodernism*, edited by L. Nicholson, 39–62. New York; London: Routledge.

Fox, G. L. (1977). '"Nice Girl": Social Control of Women Through a Value Construct'. *Signs* 2 (4): 805–817.

Freedman, J. (2007). *Gendering the International Asylum and Refugee Debate*. New York: Palgrave Macmillan.

Gale, L. A. (2006). 'Livelihoods in the Region: Sustaining Relationships Across Borders: Gendered Livelihoods and Mobility Among Sierra Leonean Refugees'. *Refugee Survey Quarterly* 25 (2): 69–80.

Gardner, J. and J. El-Busra (2016). 'The Impact of War on Somali Men, and Its Effects on the Family, Women and Children'. Rift Valley Institute Briefing Paper, February, The Rift Valley Institute, Nairobi.

Gaynor, T. (2018). 'Monsoon Rains Highlight Needs of Rohingya Refugees'. https://www.unhcr.org/news/stories/2018/7/5b34ffb64/monsoon-rains-highlight-needs-rohingya-refugees.html. Accessed 1 July 2018.

Geertz, C. (2000). *Available Light: Anthropological Reflections on Philosophical Topics.* Princeton: Princeton University Press.

Ghorashi, H. (2008). 'Giving Silence a Change: The Importance of Life Stories for Research on Refugees'. *Journal of Refugee Studies* 21 (1): 117–132.

Giddens, A. (1979). *Central Problems in Social Theory: Action, Structure and Contradiction in Social Analysis.* London: Macmillan.

———. (1991). *Modernity and Self-Identity: Self and Society in the Late Modern Age.* Stanford: Stanford University Press.

Giles, W., G. Moussa, and P. Van Esterik (eds.). (1996). *Development and Diaspora: Gender and the Refugee Experience.* Dundas, ON: Artemis.

Goodman, J. H. (2004). 'Coping with Trauma and Hardship Among Unaccompanied Refugee Youths from Sudan'. *Qualitative Health Research* 14 (9): 1177–1196.

Grabska, K. (2010). *In-Flux: (Re)negotiations of Gender, Identity and 'Home' in Post-War Southern Sudan.* PhD Dissertation, University of Sussex.

———. (2011). 'Constructing "Modern Gendered Civilised" Women and Men: Gender-Mainstreaming in Refugee Camps'. *Gender and Development* 19 (1): 81–93.

———. (2014). *Gender, Home and Identity: Nuer Repatriation to Southern Sudan.* Oxford: Boydell & Brewer.

Green, P., T. MacManus, and A. Venning. (2015). 'Countdown to Annihilation: Genocide in Myanmar'. *International State Crime Initiative.* http://statecrime.org/state-crime-research/isci-report-countdown-to-annihilation-genocide-in-myanmar/. Accessed 15 December 2016.

Greenhouse, C. J., E. Mertz, and K. B. Warren (eds.). (2002). *Ethnography in Unstable Places: Everyday Lives in Contexts of Dramatic Political Change.* Durham: Duke University Press.

Gren, N. (2015). *Occupied Lives: Maintaining Integrity in a Palestinian Refugee Camp in the West Bank.* Cairo: American University in Cairo Press.

Grønlund, C. A. (2016). *Refugees in Exodus: Statelessness and Identity – A Case Study of Rohingya Refugees in Aceh, Indonesia*. Master's thesis, University of Agder.

Grossberg, L. (2000). 'History, Imagination and the Politics of Belonging: Between the Death and the Fear of History'. In *Without Guarantees: In Honour of Stuart Hall*, edited by P. Gilroy, L. Grossberg, and A. McRobbie, 148–164. London: Verso.

Gupta, A. and J. Ferguson (eds.). (1997). *Culture, Power, Place: Explorations in Critical Anthropology*. Durham: Duke University Press.

Hackett, B. N. (1996). *Pray God and Keep Walking: Stories of Women Refugees*. London: McFarland.

Hajdukowski-Ahmed, M., N. Khanlou, and H. Moussa. (2008). *Not Born a Refugee Woman: Contesting Identities, Rethinking Practices*. New York: Berghahn.

Hall, S. (1991). 'Ethnicity: Identity and Difference'. *Radical America* 2 (4): 9–20.

Hammersley, M. (1995). *The Politics of Social Research*. London: Sage Publications.

Hammond, L. (2004). *This Place Will Become Home*. Ithaca: Cornell University Press.

Hans, A. (2012). 'Of Displacement and Gendered Spaces: A Note'. *Peace Prints: South Asian Journal of Peacebuilding* 4 (1): 1–11.

Haraway, D. (1988). 'Situated Knowledges: The Science Question in Feminism and the Privilege of Partial Perspective'. *Feminist Studies* 14 (3): 575–599.

Harding, S. (1987). *Feminism and Methodology*. Bloomington: Indiana University Press.

Hartsock, N. (1983). 'The Feminist Standpoint: Developing the Ground from a Specifically Feminist Historical Materialism'. In *Discovering Reality*, edited by S. Harding and M. Hintikka, 283–310. London: D. Riedel Publishing.

Hearn, J. and W. Parker. (2001). *Gender, Sexuality and Violence in Organizations*. London: Sage Publications.

Highmore, Ben. (2011). *Ordinary Lives: Studies in the Everyday*. London: Routledge.

Hindstrom, H. (2012). 'Burma's Monks Call for Muslim Community to be Shunned'. *The Independent*. http://www.independent.co.uk/news/world/asia/burmas-monks-call-for-muslim-community-to-be-shunned-7973317.html. Accessed 23 February 2017.

Holt, M. (2015). 'An "Invented People": Palestinian Refugee Women and Meanings of Home'. *An International E-Journal for Critical Geographies* 14 (2): 98–106.

Hondagneu-Sotelo, P. (2000). 'Feminism and Migration'. *Annals of the American Academy of Political and Social Science* 571 (1): 107–120.

Human Rights Watch. (2015). 'Southeast Asia: Accounts from Rohingya Boat People'. https://www.hrw.org/news/2015/05/27/southeast-asia-accounts-rohingya-boat-people. Accessed 13 January 2017.

———. (2018). '"Bangladesh Is Not My Country": The Plight of Rohingya Refugees from Myanmar'. https://www.hrw.org/report/2018/08/05/bangladesh-not-my-country/plight-rohingya-refugees-myanmar. Accessed 5 August 2018.

Huseby-Darvas, E. V. (1994). '"But Where Can We Go?" Refugee Women in Hungary from the Former Yugoslavia'. In *Selected Papers on Refugee Issues: III*, edited by A. Zaharlick and J. MacDonald, 63–77. Arlington: American Anthropological Association.

Hyndman, J. (2007). 'The Securitization of Fear in Post-Tsunami Sri Lanka'. *Annals of the Association of American Geographers* 97 (2): 361–372.

Hyndman, J., and M. de Alwis. (2003). 'Beyond Gender: Towards a Feminist Analysis of Humanitarianism and Development in Sri Lanka'. *Women's Studies Quarterly* 31 (3–4): 212–226.

———. (2004). 'Bodies, Shrines, and Roads: Violence, (im)Mobility and Displacement in Sri Lanka'. *Gender, Place and Culture* 11 (4): 535–557.

Ibrahim, A. (2016). *The Rohingyas: Inside Myanmar's Hidden Genocide*. London: Hurst.

Indra, D. (ed.). (1998). *Engendering Forced Migration: Theory and Practice*. New York: Berghahn.

Jackson, M. (2013). *The Politics of Storytelling: Violence, Transgression and Intersubjectivity*. Copenhagen: Museum Musculanum Press.

Jagger, G. (2008). *Judith Butler: Sexual Politics, Social Change and the Power of the Performative*. New York: Routledge.

Johnson, P. (2010). 'Unmarried in Palestine: Embodiment and (dis)Empowerment in the Lives of Single Palestinian Women'. *IDS Bulletin* 41 (2): 106–115.

Julian, R. (1997). 'Invisible Subjects and the Victimized Self: Settlement Experiences of Refugee Women in Australia'. In *Gender and Catastrophe*, edited by R. Lentin, 196–210. London: Zed Books.

Kabeer, N. (2005). 'Gender Equality and Women's Empowerment: A Critical Analysis of the Third Millennium Development Goal'. *Gender and Development* 13 (1): 13–24.

Kaiser, T. (2008). 'Social and Ritual Activity In and Out of Place: The "Negotiation of Locality" in a Sudanese Refugee Settlement'. *Mobilities* 3 (3): 375–395.

———. (2010). 'Dispersal, Division and Diversification: Durable Solutions and Sudanese Refugees in Uganda'. *Journal of Eastern African Studies* 4 (1): 44–60.

————. (2016). 'Risk and Social Transformation: Gender and Forced Migration'. In *Handbook on Gender and War*, edited by S. Sharoni, J. Welland, L. Steiner, and J. Pedersen, 194–212. Cheltenham: Edward Elgar.

Kandiyoti, D. (1988). 'Bargaining with Patriarchy'. *Gender and Society* 2 (3): 274–290.

Kawachi, I. and L. F. Berkman. (2001). 'Social Ties and Mental Health'. *Journal of Urban Health: Bulletin of the New York Academy of Medicine* 78 (3): 458–467.

Khawaja, N. G., K. M. White, R. Schweitzer, and J. Greenslade. (2008). 'Difficulties and Coping Strategies of Sudanese Refugees: A Qualitative Approach'. *Transcultural Psychiatry* 45 (3): 489–512.

Kibreab, G. (1993). 'Myth of Dependency Among Camp Refugees in Somalia 1979–1989'. *Journal of Refugee Studies* 6 (4): 321–349.

Kim, S. K. (2014). '"I Am Well-Cooked Food": Survival Strategies of North Korean Female Border-Crossers and Possibilities for Empowerment'. *Inter-Asia Cultural Studies* 15 (4): 553–571.

Kojima, Y. (2015). 'Rohingya Women in Migration: Lost Voices'. *Our World: United Nations University.* https://ourworld.unu.edu/en/rohingya-women-in-migration-lost-voices. Accessed 7 January 2017.

La Barbera, M. (2015). 'Identity and Migration: An Introduction'. In *Identity and Migration in Europe: Multidisciplinary Perspectives*, edited by M. La Barbera, 1–13. London: Springer.

Letchamanan, H. (2013). 'Myanmar's Rohingya Refugees in Malaysia: Education and the Way Forward'. *Journal of International and Comparative Education* 2 (2): 86–97.

Lorber, J. (1994). *Paradoxes of Gender.* New Haven: Yale University Press.

Lubkemann, S. C. (2002). 'Refugees: Worldwide Displacement and International Response'. *AnthroNotes* 23 (2): 1–11.

Mackinnon, C. (1998). 'Rape, Genocide, and Women's Human Rights'. In *Violence Against Women: Philosophical Perspectives*, edited by S. French, W. Teays, and L. M. Purdy, 43–54. Ithaca: Cornell University Press.

Mahler, S. J. and P. R. Pessar. (2006). 'Gender Matters: Ethnographies Bring Gender from the Periphery toward the Core of Migration Studies'. *International Migration Review* 40 (1): 27–63.

————. (2010). 'Gendered Geographies of Power: Analyzing Gender Across Transnational Spaces'. *Identities* 7 (4): 441–459.

Mahmood, S. (2001). 'Theory, Embodiment and the Docile Agent: Some Reflections on the Egyptian Islamic Revival'. *Cultural Anthropology* 6 (2): 202–236.

————. (2005). *Politics of Piety: The Islamic Revival and the Feminist Subject*. Princeton: Princeton University Press.

Mahmood, S. S., E. Wroe, A. Fuller, and J. Leaning. (2016). 'The Rohingya People of Myanmar: Health, Human Rights, and Identity'. *The Lancet* 389 (10081): 1841–1850.

Malkki, L. (1995). *Purity and Exile: Violence, Memory, and National Cosmology among Hutu Refugees in Tanzania*. Chicago; London: The University of Chicago Press.

Matheson, K., S. Jorden, and H. Anisman. (2008). 'Relations Between Trauma Experiences and Psychological, Physical and Neuroendocrine Functioning Among Somali Refugees: Mediating Role of Coping and Acculturation Stressors'. *Journal of Immigrant and Minority Health* 10 (4): 291–304.

Mazzucato, V. (2009). 'Bridging Boundaries with a Transnational Research Approach'. In *Ethnography: Theory, Praxis, and Locality in Contemporary Research*, edited by M. A. Falzon, 215–232. Surrey: Ashgate Publishing.

McDowell, L. (1999). *Gender, Identity and Place: Understanding Feminist Geographies*. Cambridge: Polity Press.

Mcdowell, R. and M. Mason. (2014). 'Desperate Rohingya Children Flee Myanmar Alone by Boat'. *The National*. http://www.thenational.ae/world/southeast-asia/desperate-rohingya-children-flee-mynamar-alone-by-boat. Accessed 11 March 2017.

McMichael, C. (2002). 'Everywhere Is Allah's Place: Islam and the Everyday Life of Somali Women in Melbourne, Australia'. *Journal of Refugee Studies* 15 (2): 171–188.

McNamara, P. (2009). 'Feminist Ethnography: Storytelling that Makes a Difference'. *Qualitative Social Work* 8 (2): 161–177.

McSpadden, L. A. and H. Moussa. (1993). 'I Have a Name: The Gender Dynamics in Asylum and in Resettlement of Ethiopian and Eritrean Refugees in North America'. *Journal of Refugee Studies* 6 (3): 203–225.

Meertens, D. and N. Segura-Escobar. (1997). 'Uprooted Lives: Gender, Violence and Displacement in Colombia'. *Singapore Journal of Tropical Geography* 17 (2): 165–178.

Mehta, A. (2017). *Right-Wing Sisterhood: Everyday Politics of Hindu Nationalist Women in India and Zionist Settler Women in Israel-Palestine*. PhD dissertation, SOAS University of London.

Merry, S. E. (2006a). *Human Rights and Gender Violence: Translating International Law in Local Justice*. Chicago: University of Chicago Press.

———. (2006b). 'Transnational Human Rights and Local Activism: Mapping the Middle'. *American Anthropologist* 108 (1): 38–51.

———. (2009). *Gender Violence: A Cultural Perspective*. West Sussex: Wiley-Blackwell.

Minh-ha, T. T. (1989). *Woman, Native, Other: Writing Postcoloniality and Feminism*. Bloomington: Indiana University Press.

Moghissi, H. (1999). 'Away from Home: Iranian Women, Displacement, Cultural Resistance and Change'. *Journal of Comparative Family Studies* 30 (2): 207–217.

Moghissi, H. (1999). 'Away from Home: Iranian Women, Displacement, Cultural Resistance and Change'. *Journal of Comparative Family Studies* 30 (2): 207–217.

Mohanty, C. T. (1991a). 'Introduction: Cartographies of Struggle, Third World Women and the Politics of Feminism'. In *Third World Women and the Politics of Feminism*, edited by C. T. Mohanty, A. Russo, and L. Torres, 1–47. Bloomington: Indiana University Press.

———. (1991b). 'Under Western Eyes: Feminist Scholarship and Colonial Discourses'. In *Third World Women and the Politics of Feminism*, edited by C. T. Mohanty, A. Russo, and L. Torres, 51–80. Bloomington: Indiana University Press.

———. (2003). *Feminism Without Borders: Decolonizing Theory, Practicing Solidarity*. Durham: Duke University Press.

Moore, H. (1986). *Space, Text and Gender: An Anthropological Study of the Marakwet of Kenya*. Cambridge: Cambridge University Press.

———. (1988). *Feminism and Anthropology*. Cambridge: Polity Press.

———. (1994). *A Passion for Difference. Essays in Anthropology and Gender*. Bloomington: Indiana University Press.

———. (1994). 'The Problem of Explaining Violence in the Social Sciences'. In *Sex and Violence: Issues in Representation and Experience*, edited by P. Harvey and P. Gow, 138–155. London: Routledge.

———. (2007). *The Subject of Anthropology: Gender, Symbolism and Psychoanalysis*. Cambridge: Polity Press.

Morawska, E. (2000). 'Intended and Unintended Consequences of Forced Migrations: A Neglected Aspect of East Europe's Twentieth Century History'. *International Migration Review* 34 (4): 1049–1087.

Mortada, S. S. (2010). 'The Notion of Women as Bearers of Culture in Monica Ali's *Brick Lane*'. *BRAC University Journal* 7 (1–2): 53–59.

Muhanna, A. (2016). *Agency and Gender in Gaza: Masculinity, Femininity, and Family during the Second Intifada*. New York: Routledge.

Narayan, U. (2004). 'The Project of Feminist Epistemology: Perspectives from a Nonwestern Feminist'. In *The Feminist Standpoint Theory Reader: Intellectual and Political Controversies*, edited by S. Harding, 213–224. New York: Routledge.

Nolin, C. (2006). *Transnational Ruptures: Gender and Forced Migration*. Aldershot: Ashgate Publishing.

Nordstrom, C. (1997). *A Different Kind of War Story (The Ethnography of Political Violence)*. Philadelphia: University of Pennsylvania Press.

Oakley, A. (1981). 'Interviewing Women: A Contradiction in Terms'. In *Doing Feminist Research*, edited by H. Roberts, 30–61. London: Routledge.

OHCHR. (2017). 'Interviews with Rohingyas Fleeing from Myanmar Since 9 October 2016'. https://www.ohchr.org/Documents/Countries/MM/FlashReport3Feb2017.pdf. Accessed 16 July 2018.

Omata, N. (2016). 'Home-making During Protracted Exile: Diverse Responses of Refugee Families in the Face of Remigration'. *Transnational Social Review* 6 (1–2): 26–40.

Omidian, P. A. (2000). 'Life Out of Context: Recording Afghan Refugees' Stories'. In *Psychosocial Wellness of Refugees: Issues in Qualitative and Quantitative Research*, edited by F. L. Ahearn, 41–66. New York: Berghahn.

Ong, A. (1988). 'Colonialism and Modernity: Feminist Representations of Women in Non-Western Societies'. *Inscriptions* 3 (4): 79–93.

———. (1995). 'Women Out of China: Traveling Tales and Traveling Theories in Postcolonial Feminism'. In *Women Writing Culture*, edited by R. Behar and D. A. Gordon, 350–372. Berkeley: University of California Press.

———. (2003). *Buddha Is Hiding: Refugees, Citizenship, the New America*. Berkeley; Los Angeles: University of California Press.

Ortner, S. B. (1996). *Making Gender: The Politics and Erotics of Culture*. Boston: Beacon Press.

Oxfam. (2019). 'Rohingya People Still Trapped Two Years on From Exodus'. https://www.oxfam.org/en/press-releases/rohingya-people-still-trapped-two-years-exodus. Accessed 23 August 2019.

Palmer, V. (2011). 'Analysing Cultural Proximity: Islamic Relief Worldwide and Rohingya Refugees in Bangladesh'. *Development in Practice* 21 (1): 96–108.

Pandya, S. (2012). *Muslim Women and Islamic Resurgence: Religion, Education, and Identity Politics in Bahrain*. London: I. B. Tauris.

Parashar, S. (2016). 'Feminism and Postcolonialism: (En)gendering Encounters'. *Postcolonial Studies* 19 (4): 371–377.

Parpart, J. L. (2010). 'Choosing Silence: Rethinking Voice, Agency, and Women's Empowerment'. Working Paper 297, Center for Gender in a Global Context, Michigan State University.

Peacock, J. (2001). *The Anthropological Lens: Harsh Light, Soft Focus*. Cambridge: Cambridge University Press.

Pedersen, J. (2016). 'In the Rain and in the Sun: Women's Peace Activism in Liberia'. In *Handbook on Gender and War*, edited by S. Sharoni, J. Welland, L. Steiner, and J. Pedersen, 400–418. Cheltenham: Edward Elgar Publishing.

Peteet, J. (2005). *Landscape of Hope and Despair: Palestinian Refugee Camps*. Philadelphia: University of Pennsylvania Press.

———. (2016). 'Camps and Enclaves: Palestine in the Time of Closure'. *Journal of Refugee Studies* 29 (2): 208–228.

Peterson, S. V. (2008). 'New Wars' and Gendered Economies'. *Feminist Review* 88: 7–20.

———. (2009). 'Gendering Informal Economies in Iraq'. In *Women and War in the Middle East: Transnational Perspectives*, edited by N. Al-Ali and N. Pratt, 35–64. New York: Zed Books.

Pink, S. (2006). *The Future of Visual Anthropology: Engaging the Senses*. New York: Routledge.

Porter, H. (2020). 'Moving Toward "Home": Love and Relationships Through War and Displacement'. *Journal of Refugee Studies* 33 (4): 813–831.

Preston, P. W. (1997). *Political/Cultural Identity: Citizens and Nations in a Global Era*. London: Sage Publications.

Rabinow, P. (1977). *Reflections on Fieldwork in Morocco*. Berkeley; Los Angeles: University of California Press.

Radcliffe, S. A. (1994). '(Representing) Postcolonial Women: Authority, Difference and Feminisms'. *Royal Geographical Society* 26 (1): 25–32.

Radhakrishnan, S. (2009). 'Professional Women, Good Families: Respectable Femininity and the Cultural Politics of a "New" India'. *Qualitative Sociology* 32 (March): 195–212.

Ragland, T. K. (1994). 'Burma's Rohingyas in Crisis: Protection of "Humanitarian" Refugees under International Law'. *Boston College Third World Law Journal* 14 (2): 300–336.

Rahman, F. (2021). '"I Find Comfort Here": Rohingya Women and *Taleems* in Bangladesh's Refugee Camps'. *Journal of Refugee Studies* 34 (1): 874–889.

Rajasingham-Senanayake, D. (2006). 'Between Tamil and Muslim: Women Mediating Multiple Identities in a New War'. In *Gender, Conflict and Migration*, edited by C. N. Behera, 175–204. London: Sage Publications.

Ramazanoglu, C. and J. Holland. (2002). *Feminist Methodology: Challenges and Choices*. London: Sage Publications.

Refugee International. (2012). *Myanmar, Bangladesh Trample on Rohingya Rights*. https://www.refugeesinternational.org/press-room/press-release/myanmar-bangladesh-trample-rohingya-rights. Accessed 10 February 2017.

Reid, C., L. Greaves, and S. Kirby. (2017). *Experience Research Social Change: Critical Methods*. Toronto: University of Toronto Press.

Reinharz, S. (1992). *Feminist Methods in Social Research*. New York: Oxford University Press.

Ripoli, S., I. Iqbal, K. F. Farzana, A. Masood, C. S. Galache, E. Mirante, A. de Chickera, et al. (2017). 'Social and Cultural Factors Shaping Health and Nutrition, Wellbeing and Protection of the Rohingya Within a Humanitarian Context'. *Social Science in Humanitarian Action Platform*, 1 (October): 1–34.

Ritchie, H. A. (2018). 'Gender and Enterprise in Fragile Refugee Settings: Female Empowerment Amidst Male Emasculation – A Challenge to Local Integration?' *Disasters* 42 (S1): S40–S60.

Robinson, I. G. and I. S. Rahman. (2012). 'The Unknown Fate of the Stateless Rohingya'. *Oxford Monitor of Forced Migration* 2 (2): 16–20.

Rodgers, G. (2004). '"Hanging Out" with Forced Migrants: Methodological and Ethical Challenges'. *Forced Migration Review* 21 (September): 48–49.

Ross, E. 'The Unspeakable Horrors Endured by the World's Most Persecuted Minority'. *VICE*. https://www.vice.com/en/article/gyxvv9/myanmar-burma-rohingya-worlds-most-persecuted-minority. Accessed 22 March 22 2018.

Rugh, A. B. (1984). *Family in Contemporary Egypt*. Syracuse: Syracuse University Press.

Sampson, R. and M. S. Gifford. (2010). 'Place-Making, Settlement and Well-Being: The Therapeutic Landscapes of Recently Arrived Youth with Refugee Backgrounds'. *Health and Place* 16 (1): 116–131.

Sayigh, R. (1994). *Too Many Enemies: The Palestinian Experience in Lebanon*. London: Zed Books.

———. (2002). 'Remembering Mothers, Forming Daughters: Palestinian Women's Narratives in Refugee Camps in Lebanon'. In *Women and the Politics of Military Confrontation*, edited by N. Abdo and R. Lentin, 56–71. New York: Berghahn.

———. (2005). 'Remembering Mothers, Forming Daughters: Palestinian Women's Narratives in Refugee Camps in Lebanon'. In *Women and Islam: Critical Concepts in Sociology*, edited by H. Moghissi, 409–426. New York: Routledge.

Scannell, L. and R. Gifford. (2010). 'Defining Place Attachment: A Tripartite Organizing Framework'. *Journal of Environmental Psychology* 30 (1): 1–10.

Scheper-Hughes, N. (2008). 'A Talent for Life: Reflections on Human Vulnerability and Resilience'. *Ethnos* 73 (1): 25–56.

Schrijvers, J. (1999). 'Fighters, Victims and Survivors: Constructions of Ethnicity, Gender and Refugeeness Among Tamils in Sri Lanka'. *Journal of Refugee Studies* 12 (3): 307–333.

Seamon, D. (2014). 'Place Attachment in Phenomenology: The Synergistic Dynamism of Place'. In *Place Attachment: Advances in Theory, Methods and Application*, edited by C. L. Manzo and P. Devine-Wright, 11–22. New York: Routledge.

Shoeb, M., H. M. Weinstein, and J. Halpern. (2007). 'Living in Religious Time and Space: Iraqi Refugees in Dearborn, Michigan'. *Journal of Refugee Studies* 20 (3): 441–460.

Sideris, T. (2001). 'Rape in War and Peace: Social Context, Gender, Power, and Identity'. In *The Aftermath: Women in Post-Conflict Transformation*, edited by S. Meintjes, A. Pillay, and M. Turshen, 46–62. London: Zed Books.

———. (2003). 'War, Gender and Culture: Mozambican Women Refugees'. *Social Science and Medicine* 56 (4): 713–724.

Simich, L. and L. Andermann (eds.). (2014). *Refuge and Resilience: Promoting Resilience and Mental Health Among Resettled Refugees and Forced Migrants*. New York: Springer.

Spivak, G. C. (1988). 'Can the Subaltern Speak?' In *Marxism and the Interpretation of Culture*, edited by L. Grossberg and C. Nelson, 271–313. Basingstoke: Macmillan Education.

Staggenborg, S., D. Eder, and L. Sudderth. (1993–1994). 'Women's Culture and Social Change: Evidence from the National Women's Festival'. *Berkeley Journal of Sociology* 38: 31–56.

Stedman, R. C. (2002). 'Toward a Social Psychology of Place: Predicting Behavior from Place Based Cognitions, Attitude, and Identity'. *Environment and Behavior* 34 (5): 561–581.

Szczepaniková, A. (2005). 'Gender Relations in a Refugee Camp: A Case of Chechens Seeking Asylum in the Czech Republic'. *Journal of Refugee Studies* 18 (3): 281–298.

———. (2006). 'Migration as Gendered and Gendering Process: A Brief Overview of the State of Art and a Suggestion for Future Directions in Migration Research'. *migrationonline.cz: Focus on Central and Eastern Europe*. http://migrationonline.cz/en/migration-as-gendered-and-gendering-process-a-brief-overview-of-the-state-of-art-and-a-suggestion-for-future-directions-in. Accessed 13 April 2017.

———. (2008). *Constructing a Refugee: The State, NGOs and Gendered Experiences of Asylum in the Czech Republic*. PhD dissertation, University of Warwick.

Taha, D. (2019). '"Seeking a Widow with Orphaned Children": Understanding Sutra Marriage Amongst Syrian Refugee Women in Egypt'. In *Migration and Islamic Ethics: Issues of Residence, Naturalization and Citizenship*, edited by R. Jureidini and F. S. Hassan, 67–91. Boston: Brill.

Tickner, J. A. (2006). 'Feminism Meets International Relations: Some Methodological Issues'. In *Feminist Methodologies for International Relations*, edited by B. A. Ackerly, M. Stern, and J. True, 19–41. Cambridge: Cambridge University Press.

Tsing, A. L. (1993). *In the Realm of the Diamond Queen: Marginality in an Out-of-the-Way Place*. Princeton: Princeton University Press.

Turner, S. (1999). 'Angry Young Men in Camps: Gender, Age and Class Relations Among Burundian Refugees in Tanzania'. UN High Commissioner for Refugees (UNHCR), Working Paper No. 9. https://www.refworld.org/reference/research/unhcr/1999/en/87299. Accessed 12 March 2017.

———. (2000). 'Vindicating Masculinity: The Fate of Promoting Gender Equality'. *Forced Migration Review* 9 (December): 8–9.

———. (2004). 'New Opportunities: Angry Young Men in a Tanzanian Refugee Camp'. In *Refugees and the Transformation of Societies: Agency, Policies, Ethics and Politics*, edited by P. Essed, G. Frerks, and J. Schrijvers, 94–105. New York; Oxford: Berghahn.

———. (2015). 'What Is a Refugee Camp? Explorations of the Limits and Effects of the Camp'. *Journal of Refugee Studies* 29 (2): 139–148.

Turton, D. (2005). 'The Meaning of Place in a World of Movement: Lessons from Long-Term Field Research in Southern Ethiopia'. *Journal of Refugee Studies* 18 (3): 258–280.

Twigger-Ross, C. L. and D. L. Uzell. (1996). 'Place and Identity Processes'. *Journal of Environmental Psychology* 16 (3): 205–220.

UNFPA. (2018). 'One Year On, Rohingya Women and Girls Seek Safety – and a Chance to Heal'. https://www.unfpa.org/news/one-year-rohingya-women-and-girls-seek-safety-%E2%80%93-and-chance-heal. Accessed 16 October 2018.

Uddin, N. (2020). *The Rohingya: An Ethnography of 'Subhuman' Life*. New Delhi: Oxford University Press.

Van Maanen, J. (2011). *Tales of the Field: On Writing Ethnography*. Chicago: The University of Chicago Press.

Vasey, K. (2011). 'Place-making, Provisional Return, and Well-being: Iraqi Refugee Women in Australia'. *Refuge: Canada's Journal on Refugees* 28 (1): 25–35.

Vera-Sanso, P. (2016). 'Taking the Long View: Attaining and Sustaining Masculinity Across the Life Course in South India'. In *Masculinities under Neoliberalism*, edited by A. Cornwall, 80–98. London: Zed Books.

Verdirame, G. and B. Harrell-Bond. (2005). *Rights in Exile: Janus-Faced Humanitarianism*. New York: Berghahn.

Visweswaran, K. (1997). 'Histories of Feminist Ethnography'. *Annual Review of Anthropology* 26 (1): 591–621.

Ward, J. and B. Vann. (2002). 'Gender-Based Violence in Refugee Settings'. *The Lancet* 360 (December): S13–S14.

Watson, G. (1987). 'Make Me Reflexive, But Not Yet: Strategies for Managing Essential Reflexivity in Ethnographic Discourse'. *Journal of Anthropological Research* 43 (1): 29–41.

West, C. and D. Zimmerman. (1987). 'Doing Gender'. *Gender and Society* 1 (2): 125–151.

Whitehead, A. (1995). '"I'm Hungry, Mum": The Politics of Domestic Budgeting'. In *The Politics of Domestic Consumption: Critical Readings*, edited by S. Jackson and S. Moores, 37–52. New York: Routledge.

Wibben, A. T. R. (ed.). (2016). *Researching War: Feminist Methods, Ethics and Politics*. New York: Routledge.

Wilde, R. (1998). 'Quis Custodiet Ipsos Custodes? Why and How UNHCR Governance of "Development" Refugee Camps Should be Subject to International Human Rights Law'. *Yale Human Rights and Development Law Journal* 1 (1): 107–128.

Winter, B. (2016). 'Women as Cultural Markers/Bearers'. In *The Wiley Blackwell Encyclopedia of Gender and Sexuality Studies*, edited by N. A. Naples, 1–5. West Sussex: Wiley-Blackwell.

Wolf, D. L. (1996). 'Situating Feminist Dilemmas in Fieldwork'. In *Feminist Dilemmas in Fieldwork*, edited by L. D. Wolf, 1–55. New York: Routledge.

Women's League of Burma. (2002). 'Breaking the Silence'. https://www.womenofburma.org/reports/breaking-silence-0. Accessed 18 May 2017.

Zarni, M. and A. Cowley. (2014). 'The Slow-Burning Genocide of Myanmar's Rohingya'. *Pacific Rim Law and Policy Journal* 23 (3): 681–752.

Index